4th

Developmental and Interpretive Manual For

The Lollipop Test:

A Diagnostic Screening Test of School Readiness-IV

By Alex L. Chew, Ed.D.

DEVELOPMENTAL AND INTERPRETIVE MANUAL FOR THE LOLLIPOP TEST: A DIAGNOSTIC SCREENING TEST OF SCHOOL READINESS - IV

(Revised and Updated Fourth Edition)

By: Alex L. Chew, Ed.D.
Professor Emeritus of Educational Psychology
and Counseling
Georgia Southern University

Rasch and Other Statistical Consultation
Contributed By:
W. Steve Lang, Ph.D.
Professor of Measurement and Research
University of South Florida

The Developmental and Interpretive Manual for the Lollipop Test
© Green Dragon Publications 2020

Humanics Test Corps. Publications are an imprint of and published by © Green Dragon Publishing.
It's trademark, consisting of the words "Humanics Psychological Test Corp." and a portrayal of a silhouetted girl, is registered in the U. S. Patent Office and in other countries.

© Green Dragon Publishing
P.O. Box 1608
Lake Worth Beach, FL 33460
Phone: (561) 533-6231 or (800) 874-8844
Fax: (561) 533-5233
Email: info@greendragonbooks.com
www.greendragonbooks.com

Printed in the Unitex States of America

Library of Congress Control Number: 2007924572

ISBN (Paperback): 0-89334-435-4 9780993344351
ISBN (Hardcover): 0-89334-436-2   9780893344368

TABLE OF CONTENTS

LIST OF TABLES

INTRODUCTION

The original idea and rationale for the development of the *Lollipop Test* evolved during this author's tenure as a school psychologist. Recent decades have seen a trend toward increasingly earlier identification of children with learning and/or adjustment problems. However, while working as a school psychologist and assessing kindergarten aged children, I found a need for a quick, yet valid, individually administered instrument for evaluation school readiness. The *Lollipop Test* was developed over a two year period to fill this void.

The initial discussions in this manual center around the concept and theory of readiness, criterion-referenced versus normed-referenced tests and how these concepts influenced the design and development of the *Lollipop Test*. The *Lollipop Test* is designed as a criterion-referenced instrument and contains specificable and teachable units of information and skills that are considered important for children entering kindergarten and/or the first grade.

This manual presents an overview of the design, development and statistical validation of the *Lollipop Test*. The initial validation (standardization) study is presented in considerable detail. Two follow-up research studies are also outlined: a follow-up to the original standardization study, using a larger number of subjects; and a validation study with pre-kindergarten subjects using the same student record booklet, comparison of beginning and ending scores, and documentation of student mastery of essential readiness skills. Additional follow-up research outlined includes validation and predictive studies. The predictive validation research includes both a two year and a significant four year longitudinal study. Additional studies conducted since the previous edition of this manual report validation information concerning the Spanish language edition. Several examples of norms tables are presented as a result of recent, on-going *Lollipop Test* research. These tables might be utilized by local programs and serve as models for their norms development.

The *Administration and Scoring Booklet for the Lollipop Test* has been revised to accommodate the recording of both pre- and post-kindergarten or pre-school assessment scores. This new format allows: pre- and post-testing using the same student record booklet, comparison of beginning and ending scores, and documentations of student mastery of essential readiness skills. However, this fourth revised edition retains the original criterion-referenced approach to assessment and its colorful and interesting presentation of readiness tasks. The test items have remained the same, which means the previous research and statistical studies continue to be relevant and valid.

THE CONCEPT AND THEORY OF READINESS

In recent years the concept of readiness has come to occupy a prominent place in educational theory. Textbooks on educational psychology and child growth and development usually include sections--and sometimes whole chapters--devoted to "readiness for learning" and similar topics. It is interesting to note that the term "readiness" does not appear in the *Educational Index* prior to the 1935-38 volume and the term "school readiness" does not appear in *Psychological Abstracts* until Index 49 in 1973. However, a 2006 search of ERIC for "school readiness" produced 1,896 hits.

Great impetus was given to the general study of reading readiness by the publication in 1925 of the *Twenty-fourth Yearbook of the National Society for the Study of Education.* According to Blair and Jones (1960), this book recognized the problem of reading readiness and suggested methods of diagnosing and remedying deficiencies in readiness. Perhaps the first major experimental study of reading readiness was a doctoral dissertation written by E. C. Deputy (1930). He developed a formula for predicting first grade reading achievement from scores on various types of tests.

The concept of readiness can be related to achievement in various school subjects and at various levels of the curriculum. "Traditionally, however, readiness refers to the intellectual and social characteristics of kindergarten and first grade children. Readiness may be defined as a general responsiveness to instruction or as specific intellectual abilities that are predictive of the development of reading or of arithmetic skills" (Leton & Rutter, 1973, p. 293).

Readiness as defined by Ausubel (1959, p. 247) refers to "the adequacy of existing capacity in relation to the demands of a given learning task." "Generally, readiness refers to the capacity for meeting successfully certain expectancies or for achieving particular levels of performance" (Brandt, 1971). Even if we think of readiness only as capacity, Brandt suggests that at least three different, though interrelated, kinds of readiness stand out as especially important. One is physical maturity, which has long been recognized as a precursor to jumping, skipping, bicycling and other gross motor activities of early childhood. Physical maturity is also related to various intellectual activities and school accomplishments.

The second kind of readiness is socio-economical, having to do with developing personality qualities and the strides already taken toward independence. Kindergarteners who are relatively and outgoing and self-assured are apt to find the school world exciting and enjoyable. The dependent, withdrawn child, on the other hand, is at a different stage of development and initially needs the warm assurance and helping hand which good schools offer before other horizons can be fully developed.

The third kind of readiness discussed by Brandt might be labeled intellectual-educational, referring to the fact that during the first years of life children have already had many experiences that shape their thinking and fill their minds. By age 6 their vocabulary averages well over 2,500 words, although culturally deprived children may know only half of this number.

In the Encyclopedia of Educational Research, 4th edition, Tyler (1969) offers an indepth, concise review of the literature on the concept of readiness. In a similar earlier paper, Tyler (1964) presents a discussion of issues related to readiness to learn. The idea of readiness has been and still is inherent in our thinking about education, although Tyler's review suggests that there is considerable diversity of opinion about both practice and theory. Different theorists have different notions about the nature of child development. Some--for instance, Gesel--consider that it is a matter of maturation forces, experiences, formal and informal teaching, and equilibration--i.e., the organization of knowledge occasioned by the appearance of contradictions in the child's system of beliefs. Still others, e.g., learning psychologists, regard it as a matter of accumulating new behavior through learning from experiences.

To briefly summarize Tyler's review, there appears to be evidence in the literature of a trend away from a strict maturational view of readiness, made so popular by Gesell and his followers, toward a view of readiness which takes into account the child's environmental experiences. Readiness as seen by many in the literature is manipulative and teachable. Readiness is being manipulated and established. It is not always regarded as a state that will appear through the natural processes of an unfolding. If readiness is thought of as some condition other than some "maturational" state, then it becomes possible to propose instructional programs and materials and educational opportunities that will produce the appropriate cognitive structures or state of readiness. Others, following Piaget, are basing their theories of readiness as being influenced by both internal and external stimulation.

Hunt & Kirk (1974), for example, view the maturational conception of readiness as no longer tenable. They postulate that maturation and learning are far less separate in development than previously imagined and probably differ only conceptually. They view development as a process on ongoing, organism-environment interaction in which both the genes and adaptions to the environment are important. Similarly, Brenner (1967) says that there is a constant interaction and transaction between a child's organism and his physical, intellectual, emotional, social, economic and cultural environment, which produce his specific life experiences and his unique pattern of growth and readiness or unreadiness. Readiness then, according to Brenner (1967), can be considered a continuing function of perceptual-conceptual and personal development. The developmental approach to readiness tells and gives reasons that no two children are exactly alike; no two children arrive at readiness or unreadiness through exactly the same route or with the same speed.

Brenner postulates that each child is a unique organism of body and mind, a product of activating and activated hereditary factors. There is constant interaction and transaction between a child's organism and his physical, intellectual, emotional, social, economic and cultural environment, which produce his specific life experiences and unique patter of growth and readiness or unreadiness.

CRITERION-REFERENCED APPROACH
TO SCHOOL READINESS ASSESSMENT

Hunt & Kirk (1974) have developed a series of illustrative criterion-referenced tests of school readiness. These tests are designed around what Hunt says are teacher expectations that the children who come to them already understand the words for such perceptual abstractions as color, position, shape, and numbers; have words for them in their own vocabularies; and can easily communicate such information. He further states that various investigators, e.g., Bereiter & Engelmann (1966), have uncovered a serious lack of opportunities to acquire representational competence for such information to be common in families of poverty.

It is pointed out by Hunt and Kirk that it was Robert Glaser who in the early 1930's elaborated the requirements for measuring the learning outcomes in instructional technology and differentiated "criterion-referenced" tests from "norm-referenced" tests. According to these authors, the goal of criterion-referenced tests is to use items of information specifically related to the effects of instruction, to determine whether the individual has acquired the specific items of information, of strategies in information-processing, of motivation, and of motor skill, in which he is being instructed. The criterion-of-reference derives from the goal of the instruction. Constructing items for such a test is a matter of finding test-tasks relevant to this goal. Performance on such test items tells whether the individual student has finished this specific learning task for which the items are a criteria of mastery.

The tests developed by Hunt and Kirk are perceptual, spoken, and listening identification and of communication for the semantic domains of color, position, shape and number illustrate the possibilities for criterion-referenced tests of school readiness.

Hunt and Kirk assert in their paper that the psychometric tradition of norm-referenced testing has tended to remove testing from teaching and to diminish the degree to which testing can guide teaching. They emphasize the need for tests of specifiable and teachable units of information, information-processing strategies, motivation and values. They have demonstrated the extension of the traditional domain for criterion-referenced tests from specific learning tasks to school readiness by utilizing as criteria items of information and skill that teachers of children entering school commonly take for granted.

DESIGN AND DEVELOPMENT OF THE *LOLLIPOP TEST*

The *Lollipop Test* consists of three components: (1) a set of seven **Stimulus Cards**, (2) the **Administration and Scoring Booklet**, and (3) the ***Developmental and Interpretive Manual***. The Stimulus Cards are used with the combination Administrative and Scoring Booklet. The test contains four sections or subtests: Test 1: Identification of colors and shapes, and copying shapes; Test 2: Picture description, position, and spatial recognition; Test 3: Identification of numbers, and counting; and Test 4: Identification of letters, and writing.

The combination **Administration and Scoring Booklet** is designed in a single unit containing directions for administration, scoring instructions and criteria, space for recording pre- and post-test scores, and general interpretations guidelines. The cover sheet provides a summary of the child's scores for quick, easy reference. The author felt this design to be an improvement over tests requiring the manipulation of a separate manual and answer booklet. The **Administration and Scoring Booklet** can be filed in the child's cumulative folder for convenient future reference.

The **Developmental and Interpretive Manual** contains information on the development and validation of the *Lollipop Test*. This manual contains summaries of research and statistical analysis of the English, Spanish and French editions of the test. Interpretive guidelines and suggestions are explained. Sample norms tables for various chronological ages and testing options are included. These tables represent results from actual research studies. For the reader who is interested in comprehensive research findings, the manual also includes a chronological listing of *Lollipop Test* research and an extensive bibliography.

A complete review of the literature consulted in developing the test can be found in Chew (1977). An effort was made to include test items which would measure selected factors identified by Telegdy (1974) and Sassenrath & Maddux (1973) in their factoral analyses of school readiness tests. In general, these studies found that individual readiness tests, and readiness assessment batteries, may contain several subtests which measure similar skills or abilities. A frequent conclusion drawn from these factoral studies was the suggestion that a shorter readiness test could be developed to measure a number of the same factors measured by some batteries containing as many as 19 subtests.

The observations of Silberberg, Silberberg & Iverson (1972), and Silberberg, Iverson, & Silberberg (1968) were also considered in the development of the *Lollipop Test*. They found that the ability to recognize letters and numbers in kindergarten was highly predictive of end of first grade achievement. An effort was also made to include test items that would tap the various semantic domains of color, position, shape and number, as discussed by Hunt and Kirk (1974). On the *Lollipop Test* the examinee is required to demonstrate listening identification (decoding) by touching or pointing to items as directed by the examiner. Spoken identification (encoding) is demonstrated by the examinee through naming items in an order indicated by the examiner supplemented with simple verbal directions. Perceptual identification is required through the test.

The findings of Ilg & Ames (1965), as discussed in *School Readiness*, were reviewed in determining appropriate tasks for copying forms. They suggest that copying forms is the most reliable indicator of a child's behavioral maturity.

The literature was further investigated in order to identify the types of tasks utilized on a number of widely used readiness assessment instruments. A detailed discussion of these tests is found in Chew (1977). The types of tasks finally included in the design of the *Lollipop Test*, e.g., color recognition, copying shapes, identification of relevant details, position and spatial relations, number concepts, and symbol recognition, are also included on most of the readiness tests examined by this author. Additionally, the tasks comprising the *Lollipop Test* are specifiable and teachable units of information and skills that teachers of children entering school consider important (and often take for granted), thus the criterion-referenced emphasis of the *Lollipop Test*.

The *Lollipop Test* was designed and developed to meet the following additional criteria:

1) The test is short in length, requiring approximately 15 minutes for administering and scoring.
2) Requires only a brief orientation period for the novice examiner.
3) Designed with stimulus items, such as lollipops and kittens, which are familiar to all children regardless of socioeconomic background. In other words, the test was designed to be as cultural-free as possible. Research, which is cited in this manual, demonstrates that this objective was achieved.
4) The format is designed to be interesting to children.
5) Has diagnostic qualities.
6) Is amendable to local norming.
7) And, more recently, the revised edition has been designed to accommodate the recording of two sets of scores (pre- and post-testing).

Initial Validation (Standardization) Study
(Chew, 1977)

Abstract

The purpose of the design and development of the *Lollipop Test: A Diagnostic Screening Test of School Readiness* (the *Lollipop Test*) was to determine if such a test could be designed to have concurrent validity with a widely used instrument, e.g., the *Metropolitan Readiness Tests* (MRT), with the view to substituting the test for the instrument and/or utilizing the test as part of a readiness assessment battery.

The sample utilized in the validation study was comprised of 69 kindergarten and Head Start students (35 males and 34 females), with a mean age of 69.94 months. Each student was administered the *Lollipop Test*, the MRT, and was rated by his teacher on the Liker-type, researcher-designed Teacher Rating Scale of Readiness. Descriptive statistics, including means, medians, and standard deviations, were computed for each set of test scores and teacher ratings.

Pearson's r was used to determine the relationship between the instruments utilized in the validation study and to establish concurrent validity between the *Lollipop Test* and the MRT. The *Lollipop Test* total score was found to be highly positively correlated to the MRT total test score ($r = .86$; $p < .001$). There was also a significant positive relationship between *Lollipop Test* scores and teacher ratings. The reliability coefficient of the *Lollipop Test* was determined through use of the Kuder-Richardson formula 20 to be .93.

In a factor analysis of the *Lollipop Test,* four factors were identified as follows: Factor I--Visual-Perceptual Abilities, Factor II--Numerical Ability, Factor III--Color Recognition and/or Visual Discrimination, and Factor IV--Position and Spatial Recognition. The largest number of test items had their highest loading under the factor measuring visual-perceptual abilities. The *Lollipop Test* and the MRT share a strong orientation to visual-perceptual abilities.

The development and validation of the *Lollipop Test* demonstrates that an individually administered screening test of school readiness, which takes approximately 15 minutes to administer and score, designed to be interesting to children of varying socioeconomic backgrounds, criterion-referenced, amendable to local norming, and inexpensive to utilize, can be designed to have validity with a widely used test of proven predictive validity, e.g., the MRT.

The data used in the validation study of the *Lollipop Test* were collected from kindergarten and Head Start students who would be eligible to enter the first grade in the fall of 1977. The sample of 69 students was drawn from a population of 215 eligible students enrolled in five schools located in four northern Mississippi counties.

The mean age of the sample was 69.94 months and the median age was 69.80 months. Of the 69 kindergarten and Head Start students comprising the sample, 35 were male (17 white and 18 nonwhite) and 34 were female (18 white and 16 nonwhite). The mean number of months enrolled in kindergarten at the time of testing was 7.24 and the median was 7.52.

Each student in the sample was administered the *Lollipop Test*, the *Metropolitan Readiness Tests* (MRT), 1969 Edition, and was rated by his teacher on readiness skills using a researcher-designed Likert-type scale, which was designed for this purpose.

The Pearson Product-Moment Correlation, as outlined by Nie et. al. in *Statistical Package for the Social Sciences* (SPSS) (1970), was used to compute the correlation between the sample's scores on the *Lollipop Test* and the MRT, and between the *Lollipop Test* and teacher ratings. The main purpose of the validation study was to establish concurrent validity between the *Lollipop Test* and the MRT.

All *Lollipop Test* subtests were found to be correlated with all MRT subtests (including total scores) at the .001 level of significance, except Lollipop Subtest 2 with MRT listening, which is significant at the .05 level. The *Lollipop Test* total score was highly positively correlated to the MRT total score ($r = .86$). The correlation coefficients between *Lollipop Test* and MRT scores are listed in Table 1.

Pearson's r was also used to determine the relationship between the sample's scores on each *Lollipop Test* subtest, and the total score, and teacher ratings. There was a significant positive relationship between the sample's *Lollipop Test* scores and teacher's ratings ($r = .58$). The correlation coefficients between the sample's *Lollipop Test* scores and teacher ratings are listed in Table 2.

TABLE 1

CORRELATION OF *LOLLIPOP TEST* WITH *METROPOLITAN READINESS TESTS*

	Lollipop Test Subtests				
	Lollipop 1	Lollipop 2	Lollipop 3	Lollipop 4	Lollipop Test Total
MRT Subtests:					
Word Meaning	.53	.47	.50	.49	.58
Listening	.46	.26*	.43	.38	.45
Matching	.51	.35	.47	.56	.58
Alphabet	.70	.55	.76	.87	.89
Numbers	.66	.58	.61	.69	.76
Copying	.52	.37	.40	.54	.55
MRT Total Test	.75	.58	.71	.80	.86

* $p < .05$; all other correlation coefficients $p < .001$.

TABLE 2

CORRELATION OF *LOLLIPOP TEST* SUBTESTS
WITH TEACHER RATINGS*

	Lollipop Test Subtests				Lollipop Test Total
	Lollipop 1	Lollipop 2	Lollipop 3	Lollipop 4	
Teacher Rating Items 1 - 5	.53				
Teacher Rating Items 6 – 14		.37			
Teacher Rating Items 15 - 19			.48		
Teacher Rating Items 20 – 25				.61	
Teacher Rating Items 1 - 25					.58
Teacher Rating Overall Readiness (Item 26)					.52

*All correlation coefficients p < .001.

Pearson's r was used to determine the relationship between the four *Lollipop Test* subtests and the total test score. These correlation coefficients are given in Table 3. Descriptive statistics of the scores obtained on this initial validation study are given in Table 4.

TABLE 3

CORRELATION OF *LOLLIPOP TEST* SUBTESTS
WITH TOTAL *LOLLIPOP TEST* SCORE*

	Lollipop 1	Lollipop 2	Lollipop 3	Lollipop 4
Lollipop Total Score	.85	.72	.88	.89

*All correlation coefficients p < .001.

TABLE 4

DESCRIPTIVE STATISTICS
FOR INITIAL VALIDATION STUDY

Descriptive Statistics	Lollipop Subtests				Lollipop Total
	Lollipop 1	Lollipop 2	Lollipop 3	Lollipop 4	
Mean	14.51	13.73	14.38	12.49	55.10
Median	14.91	14.09	16.20	14.42	58.75
Mode	17.00	17.00	17.00	18.00	65.00
Range	11.00	10.00	16.00	18.00	50.00
Standard Error	.30	.31	.50	.71	1.55
Standard Deviation	2.50	2.58	4.13	5.90	12.86

N = 69

Reliability of the *Lollipop Test*

The Kuder-Richardson formula 20, modified as discussed by Ferguson (1971), was used to determine the reliability of the *Lollipop Test*. The Kuder-Richardson formula 20 is a measure of the internal consistency or homogeneity of the test material. According to Ferguson, if the items on a test have high intercorrelations with each other and are measures of much the same attribute, then the reliability coefficient will be high.

The result Kuder-Richardson formula 20 reliability coefficient for the *Lollipop Test* was .9277 ($p < .001$).

Factor Analysis of the *Lollipop Test*

The factor structure of the *Lollipop Test* was examined, using procedures discussed by Kim in the SPSS manual (Nie et. al., 1970), in an attempt to identify the underlying factors measured by the test.

An extracted factor matrix was developed using principal factor with interactions. The first four factors, which had eigenvalues greater than 2.5, were rotated by the varimax procedure. All 49 variables (test items),[1] with the exception of 18, 23, and 33, loaded on one of the four factors at values higher than .30.

The four factors were identified by this researcher as follows:

---

[1] Three test items—12, 13 and 20—were initially excluded of lack of variance.

10

Factor I: Visual-Perceptual Abilities. This factor seems to measure a child's ability to recognize symbols, including, letters, numbers, and shapes.

Factor II: Numerical Ability. This factor appears to measure a child's ability to count and, to a lesser extent, to recognize and identify numbers and shapes.

Factor III: Color Recognition and/or Visual Discrimination. This factor appears to measure the child's ability to discriminate between the basic, primary colors and to a lesser extent, to discriminate between numbers and shapes.

Factor IV: Position and Spatial Recognition. This factor seems to measure the child's ability to discriminate between the position of objects in space.

The number and letter items on the *Lollipop Test* may need special explanation. These items propose to measure number and letter knowledge by asking the subject to either point to the letter or number by the examiner or to name the letter or number pointed to by the examiner. These items are probably measuring a combination of knowledge of letters and numbers and visual perceptual abilities.

Interestingly, the literature (Telegdy, 1974) revealed the MRT to be oriented strongly to visual-perceptual abilities. Similar findings appear to be true for the *Lollipop Test*. This may be one explanation for the high positive correlation between the *Lollipop Test* and the MRT.

ADDITIONAL VALIDATION STUDIES

Validation of the *Lollipop Test* Using the MRT as the Criterion
(Chew & Morris, 1984)

Abstract

The validity of the *Lollipop Test: A Diagnostic Screening Test of School Readiness* was examined using the *Metropolitan Readiness Tests* (MRT), Level I, Form Q (1976 Edition), as the criterion. The sample of 293 kindergarten students was administered the MRT by their teachers in classroom groups; the *Lollipop Test* was individually administered by qualified examiners. All correlations across the test batteries were significant (p < .001), demonstrating appreciable concurrent validity between the MRT and the *Lollipop Test*. Further, a canonical correlation indicated a high degree of multivariate relationship between the tests. The *Lollipop Test* also offers a potentially less threatening experience for kindergarten students by providing familiar stimulus items in an individual administration format. It would appear to be particularly appropriate for children with learning or adjustment problems for whom group tests may inhibit maximum performance due to their length or the cultural bias of their items.

In a follow-up to the initial standardization study (Chew, 1977); Chew & Morris (1984) conducted a validation study of the *Lollipop Test*, which has been published in *Educational and Psychological Measurement, 44,* 987-991. A paper outlining the results of the study was presented at the Georgia Educational Research Association Meeting at the University of Georgia, Athens, Georgia, November 19, 1983 (Chew, 1983). The following is a discussion of the procedures and results of the study.

The purpose of this study was to further validate the *Lollipop Test* in regard to some of the difficulties inherent in the large scale screening of kindergarten students. These may include the amount of time involved in test administration and the need to tap the optimum potential of children who may deviate from the typical middle class child. Children from socioeconomically deprived homes, who are shy or withdrawn, or have certain learning difficulties, i.e., preservation or a short attention span, often have difficulty following test directions in a group administration and are additionally threatened by the nature of some of the tests. These factors may add to the child's test anxiety and interfere with optimum performance.

Instruments

The *Lollipop Test* is an individually administered test of school readiness with a reported total test KR-20 reliability of .93 for the standardization sample (Chew, 1981). The *Lollipop Test* is described in considerable detail elsewhere in this manual. The test is short, requiring only approximately 15 minutes for administration and scoring. Design of the test was guided by a desire to use stimuli that are very general and thus familiar to all children regardless of socioeconomic background, and to provide diagnostic help for the professional for planning and remediation strategies. Children have repeatedly demonstrated that they find the test non-threatening, fun and interesting. In addition, validity for the Lollipop Test was supported by the high correlation of its scores with teacher ratings (Chew, 1981).

The 1976 edition of the MRT, as with the earlier editions, is designed to measure readiness for first grade. Total test reliabilities for the earlier versions have been reported as generally above .90 (Dykstra, 1972). In addition, studies or earlier editions of the MRT indicated predictive validity, as it was a good predictor of first grade success (Bolig & Fletcher, 1973; Lessler & Bridges, 1973). In contrast to the *Lollipop Test,* total testing time of the MRT is 80 minutes and three or four administration sessions are recommended.

Procedures

The sample of 293 kindergarten students (159 males, 134 females; 203 whites, 89 blacks) constituted the entire public school kindergarten of a rural South Georgia county who would be eligible to enter the first grade the next fall. The mean number of months enrolled in kindergarten at the time of testing was 8.6 months, and the mean age was 74.4 months. During the first two weeks of May, each student in the sample was administered the MRT, Level 1, Form Q, by their teacher in classroom groups. During this same testing period, each student was individually administered the *Lollipop Test* by one of six qualified psychological evaluators. Classes were heterogeneous and were selected at random. Teachers were asked not to send the individual children in any particular order, e.g., sex, race, or alphabetically. All students, even those who were absent on their test day, were eventually tested.

Results and Conclusions

The correlation coefficients between the *Lollipop Test* and MRT scores are shown in Table 5. All *Lollipop Test* scores were significantly ($p < .001$) correlated with all MRT scores. The *Lollipop Test* total score is highly positively correlated to the MRT total score ($r = .76$). Letter Recognition on the MRT was highly positively related to Letters and Writing on the Lollipop Test ($r = .76$); as was Quantitative Language on the MRT and Numbers and Counting on the *Lollipop Test* ($r = .62$). In addition, the correlation of .76 between the total *Lollipop Test* and total MRT scores was especially impressive as the theoretical limit for this correlation given the tests' reported reliabilities is only about .90, with even more restriction on the subscore correlations. Further, a canonical correlation analysis produced two significant correlations ($R_1 = .82$, $R_2 = .36$, $p < .001$) indicating a high degree of multivariate relationship between the tests. These results indicated that the *Lollipop Test* has strongly concurrent validity using the MRT, a widely used test with substantiated predictive validity, as the criterion. The *Lollipop Test* also offers a potentially less threatening experience for kindergarten students by providing familiar stimulus items in an individual administration format. Kindergarten teachers, counselors and school psychologists may wish to consider the use of the *Lollipop Test* as a quick, yet reliable and valid, school readiness screening instrument.

TABLE 5

CORRELATIONS BETWEEN PART AND TOTAL SCORES ON THE *LOLLIPOP TEST* AND PART AND TOTAL SCORES ON THE *METROPOLITAN READINESS TEST**

| | MRT Subtests | | | | | | |
	1. Auditory Memory	2. Rhyming	3. Letter Recognition	4. Visual Matching	5. School Language & Listening	6. Quantitative Language Test	MRT Total
Lollipop Test Subtests:							
1. Identification of Colors, Shapes & Copying Shapes	.35	.35	.47	.44	.48	.51	.54
2. Picture Description, Position & Spatial Recognition	.39	.39	.44	.42	.47	.50	.54
3. Identification of Numbers & Counting	.48	.42	.59	.51	.49	.62	.64
4. Identification of Letters & Writing	.50	.50	.76	.52	.54	.60	.71
Lollipop Total Test	.55	.52	.73	.58	.61	.70	.76

*All correlation coefficients p < .001, df = 291.

It would appear to be particularly appropriate for children with learning or adjustment problems for whom group tests may inhibit maximum performance due to their length or the cultural bias of their items. These are some of the inherent difficulties in kindergarten screening mentioned initially in the rationale for this study.

Initial Standardization vs. Current Validation Study

In the initial standardization study of the *Lollipop Test,* Chew (1977) found the *Lollipop Test* total score was highly positively correlated to the MRT total score (r = .86, p < .001), which compares favorably with the results of this study (Chew & Morris, 1984). The following variables may help explain the difference between the two correlation coefficients. The earlier study had a sample of 69 versus 293; the 1968 edition of the MRT was used instead of the 1976 edition; and the subjects in the earlier study were administered the MRT in small groups of three students each (10 were individually tested), whereas in the present study the students were tested in class size groups. The small group and individual test administration procedure used in the earlier validation study probably reduced test error.

Validation of the Lollipop Test as a
Pre-Kindergarten Screening Instrument

(Chew & Morris, 1987)

Abstract

The validity of the *Lollipop Test: A Diagnostic Screening Test of School Readiness* was examined for a group of pre-kindergarten subjects using the *Developmental Indicator for the Assessment of Learning* (DIAL) as the criterion. This study was motivated by requests from users of the *Lollipop Test* who were interested in its validity for pre- and post-kindergarten assessment. Both the *Lollipop Test* and the DIAL were individually administered by qualified examiners to a sample of 129 pre-kindergarten pupils. The statistical significance of all the correlations ($p < .001$) between respective subtests demonstrated concurrent validity across the test batteries. Further, a canonical correlation of .84 ($p < .001$) indicates a high degree of multivariate relationship between the tests. The effects of indices related to socioeconomic status were also examined. Neither occupational level nor income level were significantly ($p < .01$) correlated with any of the subtests or total scores of either the *Lollipop Test* or the DIAL or significantly impacted any of the correlations between the two tests. As the *Lollipop Test* also appeared to overcome the limited ceiling of the DIAL, and requires fewer resources to administer, it would appear to be an attractive pre-kindergarten screening instrument.

The author has received feedback from many users of the *Lollipop Test* attesting to its usefulness as a pre- and post-kindergarten screening instrument. As noted in previously cited studies (Chew, 1981; Chew & Morris, 1984), the *Lollipop Test* has been validated as a school readiness screening instrument. These studies utilized the Metropolitan Readiness Tests as the criterion and used subjects in the closing stages of kindergarten. These criterion-related studies have been discussed in appropriate detail in this manual. However, the effectiveness of the *Lollipop Test* as a pre-kindergarten screening instrument had not been empirically investigated until a recent correlational study using the *Developmental Indicator for the Assessment of Learning* (DIAL) as the criterion. A paper reporting the results of the study was given at the Georgia Educational Research Association Meeting (Chew, 1985) and submitted to a refereed professional journal for publication (Chew & Morris, 1987). The following is a discussion of the procedures and results of the study.

Rationale/Purpose

The purpose of the study was to further validate the *Lollipop Test* as a pre-kindergarten screening instrument. The criterion used for validation was the *Developmental Indicator for the Assessment of Learning* (DIAL) (Mardell & Goldenberg, 1975), which was developed as a predictive screening battery to identify pre-kindergarten children with potential learning problems. The effects of socioeconomic status on scores obtained on the two instruments were also investigated.

Instruments

The *Lollipop Test,* which is described in great detail elsewhere in this manual, is an individually administered, criterion-referenced screening test. It is relatively short requiring only about 15 minutes for administration and scoring and utilizes stimulus items that are familiar to children of varying socioeconomic backgrounds. Due to its criterion-referenced emphasis, the test is inherently diagnostic and provides information for educational planning and remediation strategies. The total test KR-20 reliability estimate is reported in the manual as .93 (Chew, 1981). Additionally, the results of a recent validation study (Chew & Morris, 1984) demonstrated that the *Lollipop Test* has strong concurrent validity with the *Metropolitan Readiness Tests,* a widely used test with substantiated predictive validity. The DIAL is also individually administered and has been validated as a pre-kindergarten screening instrument (Obrzut, Bolocofsky, Heath, & Jones, 1981; Docherty, 1983). Obrzut et. al. (1981) employed a canonical correlation analysis to determine any significant relationships between the DIAL and MRT subtests. They conclude that the DIAL was a valid predictor of educational achievement as measured by the MRT criterion measure.

A correlational study between the two instruments seemed particularly appropriate since they both have been determined to have strong concurrent validity with the MRT, both are individually administered, and have a number of similarities and parallels among test items/tasks.

Procedures

During the second week of May, 1985, each child in the sample was individually administered the *Lollipop Test* and the DIAL by a trained examiner in the school. The sample of 129 children (70 males, 59 females; 95 whites, 34 blacks) constituted the entire group of children being screened for kindergarten the following fall. The mean chronological age at the time of testing was 62.1 months. Children were selected at random and were tested as they were brought by parents to register and be screened for kindergarten. The DIAL requires that four staff stations be established for testing. The *Lollipop Test* was simply added to the testing battery as an additional station. However, the children were not administered the battery in any particular order.

To explore the possible effects of socioeconomic factors on scores obtained on the *Lollipop Test* and the DIAL, parents were asked to complete a simple questionnaire regarding the occupation of head of household, family income range, and number of children in family. The occupational level of the head of the household was classified into one of the four ordinal categories of (1) Professional/Managerial, (2) Trade, (3) Laborer, and (4) Chronic Welfare. This phase of study was patterned after an investigation by Telegdy (1974) regarding the relationship between socioeconomic status and school readiness. Developing a test which would be non-culturally biased has been a primary objective since the earliest conceptualization of the *Lollipop Test.* Therefore, it was felt that this was an important variable to investigate.

Results and Conclusions

The correlation coefficients between the *Lollipop Test* and the DIAL are shown in Table 6. All *Lollipop Test* scores were significantly (P < .001) correlated with all DIAL scores. These between battery subtests correlations, as well as the correlation of .71 between the total scores, are especially impressive considering the probable attenuation of the correlations due to the limited validity with the DIAL criterion measure, a widely used test for pre-kindergarten screening.

Variables related to socioeconomic status were also analyzed. Unlike the findings of Telegdy (1974) for some other tests of school readiness, neither occupational level nor income level were significantly (p < .001) correlated with any of the subtests or total scores of either the *Lollipop Test* or the DIAL. Also, as evidenced by the individual partial correlations, neither occupational level nor income significantly (p < .01) impacted any of the correlations between the *Lollipop Test* and the DIAL.

A potential limitation of the DIAL in pre- and post-kindergarten screening is the large number of children who seemingly approximate the maximum scores possible during pre-kindergarten testing. This limitation was noted by Obrzut et. al. (1981) who concluded that the DIAL was not a suitable instrument for determining functioning levels for over half of the children in his sample, due to the ceiling constraints of subtests. The *Lollipop Test,* on the other hand, has a broader difficulty range, which not only provides less ceiling constraints during pre-kindergarten screening but would also allow the assessment of readiness concepts mastered during the kindergarten experience. For example, in his study the ceiling effect was evident in the DIAL as the mean total score of 74.5 was about 89% of the maximum score of 84. However, similar statistics for the *Lollipop Test* were a mean of 45.0 out of a possible 69 representing only about 65%.

TABLE 6

CORRELATIONS BETWEEN PART AND TOTAL SCORES ON THE *LOLLIPOP TEST* AND PART AND TOTAL SCORES ON THE DIAL*

	DIAL Subtests				
	1. Gross Motor	2. Fine Motor	3. Concepts	4. Communication	DIAL Total Test
Lollipop Test Scores:					
1. Identification of, Colors, Shapes & Copying Shapes	.48	.70	.69	.54	.74
2. Picture Description, Position & Spatial Recognition	.29	.53	.58	.45	.56
3. Identification of Numbers & Counting	.38	.64	.63	.39	.62
4. Identification of Letters & Writing	.27	.55	.58	.31	.52
Lollipop Total Test	.40	.71	.73	.47	.71

*All correlation coefficients p < .001, df = 125.

Docherty (1983) has also noted practical limitations to the use of the DIAL including the amount of time and personnel required. The DIAL is administered by teams of four trained professionals or paraprofessionals, each of whom gives one scale of the DIAL. The children move or rotate from one administrator to the next, with approximately six children being screened in an hour. Scoring takes place after completion of testing when all scores have been administered. Considering the time and personnel required, the limited validity information available on the DIAL, and the fact that alternative instruments in the form of teacher-completed rating scales taking about 1 minute per child may be just as effective for screening purposes, caused Docherty (1983) to question if the information obtained on the DIAL is worth the effort. The *Lollipop Test* requires only one examiner (the kindergarten teacher or a trained paraprofessional) and administration and scoring time averages 15 minutes per child.

As the *Lollipop Test* is highly predictive of the results of the DIAL, these results suggest that the *Lollipop Test* may be more useful as a pre- and post-kindergarten screening instrument than the DIAL due to the DIAL's ceiling restraint and personnel resources necessary for its administration.

As a result of this study, the *Administration and Scoring Booklet for the Lollipop Test* has been revised to accommodate the recording of pre- and post-kindergarten scores. This researcher feels that the results of the study, as well as the other validation studies cited in this manual, demonstrate the usefulness of the *Lollipop Test* in pre- and post-kindergarten assessment.

LONGITUDINAL PREDICTIVE STUDIES

Predicting Later Academic Achievement from Kindergarten Scores on the Metropolitan Readiness Tests and The *Lollipop Test*
(Chew & Morris, 1989)

Abstract

The purpose of this study was to provide further validation of the *Lollipop Test* by examining predictive validity. The study was a follow-up to the research conducted during 1981 and published several years later (Chew & Morris, 1984). In this second phase of the 1981 study, the predictive validity of the *Lollipop Test* was investigated in a longitudinal study that followed the same students, who comprised the 1981 sample, over a four-year span. Multiple regression analysis was computed for the *Lollipop Test* and the *Metropolitan Readiness Test* and the MRT grades in reading and math as the criteria. All multiple correlation coefficients for the Lollipop Test and the MRT were found to be significant and similar in magnitude. Interestingly, the relationship between these variables is slightly larger in magnitude for the *Lollipop Test* than the MRT on some first grade criteria, e.g., word reading and sentence reading on the Stanford and teacher assigned grades in reading. Perhaps especially noteworthy, was that the *Lollipop Test*, a much shorter screening instrument, performed as well as the lengthier MRT in predicting school achievement.

The study was developed in the following manner:

Rationale

The criterion-referenced (concurrent) validity of the *Lollipop Test* is well-documented in the literature. However, a predictive study of the *Lollipop Test* had not been conducted. This study made it possible to complete validity and reliability studies on the *Lollipop Test* that were begun in the initial validation (standardization) study in 1977.

The great majority of predictive validity studies utilizing the MRT and other school readiness tests have assessed learning (achievement) at the end of the first grade (Nagel 1979; Telegdy, 1975; Lessler & Bridges, 1973). This current study is especially significant in that it is a longitudinal follow-up assessing the predictive validity of the *Lollipop Test* over a span of four years.

Sample

All students included in the original kindergarten sample (Chew & Morris, 1984), who were enrolled in the school system at any time during the preceding four years were included in the sample. As a result, 246 of the original 293 students were included in some degree in the study. Because some subjects had moved since kindergarten, or were otherwise unavailable for some of the test administrations, the number of subjects available for each set of predictors and criterion varied.

Procedures

A local school system data clerk, with the system's approval, was hired to screen individual student's cumulative records to secure the necessary data for the study. This screening was completed at four individual schools within the system. The data was gathered during the Spring of 1986 for grades one through four. At that time, the majority of the students were currently enrolled in the fifth grade.

Individual student's scores in reading and math on the Stanford Achievement Test and teacher assigned grades in reading and math at the end of the first through fourth grades were recorded on data record sheets. The data was then transferred to computer disk and rechecked for accuracy.

Results and Conclusions

The multiple correlation coefficients for the *Lollipop Test* and the MRT in predicting first, third, and fourth grade achievement are shown in Table 7. All computed values were statistically significant, the majority at ($p < .001$). Although predictive accuracy generally decreased for the third and fourth grades as might be expected, all multiple correlations were significant and large enough to encourage use of these batteries for long term prediction of school achievement. Moreover, the multiple correlation coefficients for the *Lollipop Test* and the MRT were similar in magnitude at all grade levels. However, it is interesting to note that the relationship between these variables is slightly larger for the *Lollipop Test* on most first grade criteria. Generally, when examining the criteria, it appears that the *Lollipop Test* is a slightly better predictor of reading achievement and the MRT a slightly better predictor of math achievement.

In summary, both test batteries did a creditable job in predicting achievement over a span of four years. Particularly noteworthy, however, is the apparent fact that the *Lollipop Test*, a relatively brief screening instrument, holds up as well as the MRT in predicting school achievement, especially at the end of first grade. These empirical results would appear to be highly significant since the *Lollipop Test* has fewer items and requires less than one-fifth the amount of time for administration than does the MRT. The usefulness for educational implementation would appear to be obvious.

TABLE 7

MULTIPLE CORRELATIONS FROM PREDICTING FIRST, THIRD AND FOURTH GRADE ACHIEVEMENT FROM THE SUBTESTS OF THE *LOLLIPOP TEST* OR THE METROPOLITAN READINESS TESTS (MRT)

Criteria:	GRADE 1		GRADE 3		GRADE 4	
	Lollipop Test	MRT	*Lollipop Test*	MRT	*Lollipop Test*	MRT
Stanford Achievement Tests:						
Word Reading+	.75	.72				
Sentence Reading+	.63	.56				
Reading			.58	.52	.40 (N = 183)	.39
Math	.72 (N = 236)	.73	.55 (N = 227)	.68	.40 (N = 182)	.49
Teacher Assigned Grades:						
Reading Level+	.47 (N = 237)	.53				
Reading	.54 (N = 223)	.49	.42 (N = 231)	.44	.43 (N = 185)	.47
Math	.49 (N = 223)	.52	.36 (N = 234)	.45	.30 (p < .05) (N = 186)	.37 (p < .005)

Note: a) Predictors consisted of 4 subtests on the Lollipop Test and 6 subtests on the MRT.

  b) Number of subjects for each multiple correlation in parentheses.

+These criteria were used by the school system in first grade only.

All R^2 were $p < .001$, unless otherwise noted on table.

Predicting Academic Achievement in Kindergarten and First Grade From Pre-Kindergarten Scores on the *Lollipop Test*

(Chew & Lang, 1993)

Abstract

The purpose of this study was to assess the multivariate relationship of two predicators of school readiness administered four months prior to kindergarten to two groups of criteria. A sample of 110 children from rural Georgia were followed longitudinally. The overall results indicate high degree of commonality between the Developmental Indicators for the Assessment of Learning and the *Lollipop Test*. Both predictors demonstrated equivalent ability to predict students' grades and standardized test scores over two years of investigation.

Rationale

Almost four decades ago, Wendt (1979) commented on the need for prekindergarten screening and the almost nonexistent data on the predictive validity of tests used for this purpose. Accurate assessment of functioning and potential at the preschool level can help educators adopt a preventive approach to educational intervention as well as allowing for appropriate placement and remediation of deficits.

Several studies have utilized various assessment instruments prior to kindergarten to predict later academic success. Some of these studies, however, used tests that primarily assessed "intellectual potential" as opposed to general "school readiness," and did not include teacher ratings or assigned grades as a criteria. This study follows as a continuation to an earlier concurrent validity assessment of the *Lollipop Test* (Chew & Morris, 1987).

Subjects

A sample of 110 children constituted students remaining from a previous study (N=129) (Chew & Morris, 1987) enrolled in a school system during any achievement testing and/or grading period for the two years of this longitudinal study. Of the 110 participants, 60 were males and 50 were females; with 26 classified as black and 84 as white. Nineteen students did not complete the two years of the study.

Instruments and Procedures

The focus of this present study was on the multivariate relationship of two sets of predictors of school readiness (the *Lollipop Test* and the Developmental Indicators for the Assessment of Learning) administered four months prior to kindergarten to two groups of criteria (teacher grades and standardized achievement test scores).

The two standardized tests used as dependent variables were the California Achievement Test (CAT) and the Georgia Criterion Reference Test (GCRT). The CAT is a well established achievement battery which yields a scaled score.) The GCRT is a test developed by the Georgia Department of Education. The GCRT produces a scaled score for both math and reading.)

In order to maintain confidentiality of student records and ensure uniformity of data collection, each first-grade teacher was asked by the school principal to screen individual students' cumulative records to obtain the following data: (a) CAT scores in reading and math, (b) GCRT scores in reading and math, and (c) teacher-assigned grades in reading and math. Teachers were given examples of the format to be used for organizing the data. The data collection process simply became an additional step in the end of the school year cumulative records update. The data were gathered for kindergarten and first grade during post-planning at the end of the school year. The subjects were identified according to a confidential identification number.

Results and Discussion

The canonical correlations between the two sets of predictors (subtests of the Lollipop and DIAL tests) and the achievement criteria (standardized tests and teacher reported grades in math and reading) are summarized in Table 8. Overall, the results indicated a high degree of multivariate commonality between the DIAL and *Lollipop Test*. The prediction over two years time accounted for approximately 50% of achievement variance for both the DIAL and *Lollipop Test* on both standardized tests and grades. The obtained coefficient of determination (R^2) suggested that both the *Lollipop Test* and DIAL predict academic achievement in a manner consistent with literature reviews where half the variance accounted for by a single test predictor is typical.

The *Lollipop Test*, a relatively brief individual screening instrument, demonstrates almost identical prediction when compared to the longer DIAL. The predictive and concurrent validity of the *Lollipop Test* are supported by the findings in this study. Since the *Lollipop Test* has fewer items and takes less time to administer, it might be preferred in a utility comparison with the DIAL. Also, the *Lollipop Test*, as a quick individual test, appears to be useful where the child's test taking skills require individual observation or the preschooler's attention span is limited.

TABLE 8

CANONICAL CORRELATIONS BETWEEN LOLLIPOP AND DIAL SUBTESTS AND MEASURES OF ACADEMIC ACHIEVEMENT

Preschool Tests Lollipop & DIAL Subtests	Achievement	
	Standardized Tests[a]	Grades[b]
Lollipop 1 Lollipop 2 Lollipop 3 Lollipop 4	R = .7265* (X^2 = 100.7)	R = .6848* (X^2 = 98.76)
DIAL 1 DIAL 2 DIAL 3 DIAL 4	R = .7588* (X^2 = 100.7)	R = .7208* (X^2 = 98.76)
Lollipop vs. DIAL Subtests		R = .8367* (X^2 = 98.76)

[a] California Achievement Test-Math
California Achievement Test-Reading
Georgia Criterion Reference Test-Math
Georgia Criterion Reference Test-Verbal
[b] Kindergarten-Math
Kindergarten-Reading
Grade 1-Math
Grade 1-Reading

* $< .01$.

24

Predicting Academic Success of Promoted and Retained Kindergarten Students

(Lang, Chew, & Gill, 1995)

Abstract

Students enrolled in a midsize southeastern school were the initial subjects. The focus of this study was on the comparative longitudinal prediction of academic success of students from kindergarten through second grade. Fifteen variables including progress checklists, readiness tests, achievement tests, grades, and demographics were analyzed for the same students for three years. Univariate and multivariate correlational analyses were used to measure and compare the relative effectiveness of each predictor, such as a kindergarten readiness test, to each criterion, such as the ITBS in second grade. In summary, this study suggests that if one wanted to be efficient in predicting students' future grades, a short readiness test seems to be the best strategy.

Rationale

This research focus was on specific questions:

1.) What was the predictive validity of readiness testing in the early grades?
2.) Which assessment instrument has the most utility?
3.) What was the predictive validity of achievement testing?
4.) Among the subset of students who repeated kindergarten, was there evidence of later success compared to regularly promoted to students?

Unlike previous research, this design assessed academic achievement at multiple grade levels, and included teacher-assigned grades in addition to standardized academic testing. Regardless of the intervention strategy, many schools continue to retain students. Most of these students are identified by some combination of teacher recommendations, developmental checklists, readiness tests, and achievement tests. Many of these instruments have demonstrated correlation with future behavior, but they are rarely compared against each other with the same children.

Subjects

A sample of 858 students enrolled in a midsize southeastern school were the initial subjects. They were followed from kindergarten through second grade with the exception of the normal attrition each year. Of the participants, 52% were male and 48% female; 30% were white, 67% African-American, and 3% other; 57% were on free and reduced lunch. Fifty-five students repeated kindergarten before continuing to first grade during the study. Retention was primarily a function of teacher recommendation even though the various formal assessments were available.

Instruments and Procedures

Scores were obtained from the following variables: the Georgia Kindergarten Assessment Program (GKAP), the County Kindergarten/Developmental Progress Report (CPR), teacher assigned grades in mathematics and reading for each year, the *Lollipop Test: A Diagnostic Screening Test of School Readiness,* the Kindergarten California Achievement Test, The First Grade Georgia Criterion Reference Test (CRT), and the Iowa Test of Basic Skills (second grade).

In cooperation with the school district and principal, this project had access to the school's student records for the data collection. In some cases (such as with the *Lollipop Test*) the researches trained the teachers how to administer the instrument and collect data. A computerized data bank with each student's ID number was created to follow the students and maintain anonymity.

Univariate and multivariate correlational analyses were used to measure and compare the relative effectiveness of each predictor, such as a kindergarten readiness test, to each criterion, such as the ITBS in second grade. Univariate correlations probabilities were controlled using Bonferroni. Multivariate correlations were canonical. All correlational analyses were pairwise since all students did not have recorded scores for all variables. Dependent t-tests were run on readiness test scores for the retained students and independent tests were used to compare the retained students with the non-retained students.

Results and Discussion

Bivariate intercorrelation of all variables by subtest scores resulted in a 30 x 30 correlation matrix. Eliminating intercorrelations between subtests of the same instruments and including only correlations significant (p <.05 Bonferroni), produced Table 9. Also, the bivariate correlations in Table 9 could not be computed in a pairwise fashion for pairs with missing data where a class or year did not participate in one measure or another.

Canonical correlations were generated for all predictors where a set of subtests (such as Lollipop 1, Lollipop 2, Lollipop 3, and Lollipop 4) were correlated with criterion (grades, achievement test scores). Variables represented as a single score instead of a total score generated from subtests, such as the KCAT, would not differ from bivariate correlations and were excluded. This restricted the analysis to those variables available for multivariate consideration. The results are given in Table 10.

One of the most important implications of this study is the standardized readiness test vs. the progress checklist vs. achievement tests in kindergarten, which is not an uncommon battery of measurement in today's early grades. Which best predicts first and second grade success and what combinations of predictors are most useful? In this case, the Lollipop Test, the readiness instrument, the KCAT achievement test and the county and state progress checklists *all had a positive correlation* with grades in kindergarten through second. The best predictor for kindergarten grades was the progress checklist while the best overall predictor of first and second level grades was the *Lollipop Test*, followed by the KCAT achievement test. It is interesting to note that the readiness test correlations increase as the student moves from kindergarten to first to second. No single subtest value across four subtest fails to increase.

In summary, this study suggests that if one wanted to be efficient in predicting students' future grades, a short readiness test seems to be the best strategy. The *Lollipop Test* results give teachers a lesson plan to work on, can be administered in 20 minutes, and in this study provided the greatest prediction of any other single measure or combination of measures. A foregone conclusion may be that teachers can better use their valuable time teaching rather than filling out multiple progress checklists, which may not be effective predictors of future school success.

The best multivariate prediction of retention status (generally determined by teacher recommendation) was the *Lollipop Test*. The progress checklists add little or nothing to the prediction of retention status when compared to the readiness test. Since the readiness test takes 20 minutes while most of the progress checklists take hours of teacher time and piles of paper, the information is redundant as far as prediction. Based on this study, if one wanted to be efficient in predicting students' future grades and possible retention, a short readiness test seems to be the best strategy.

In an Indiana study (Eno & Woehlke, 1995), using a smaller sample (N = 161), the *Lollipop Test* successfully predicted kindergarten success and transitional first grade status, an option for children unready to succeed in a regular first-grade program. These authors concluded that the *Lollipop Test* was an excellent measure of kindergarten readiness. In a Brazilian study, Bigras & Dessen (2002) used the *Lollipop Test* as an external criteria based on their review of the related literature. They cite studies which suggested that the *Lollipop Test* appears to be a better predictor of later school success than traditional IQ measures such as the WPPSI-R.

TABLE 9

SIGNIFICANT BIVARIATE CORRELATIONS BETWEEN KINDERGARTEN PREDICTORS AND FIRST OR SECOND GRADE CRITERIA

	Grades						Test Scores				Retention in Kindergarten
Readiness Test:	Kindergarten		First		Second		First		Second		Kindergarten
							GA CRT		ITBS		
	Reading	Math	Reading	Math	Reading	Math	Reading	Math	Reading	Math	
Lollipop 1	.18	.16	.27	.29	.46	.40	.37				.26
Lollipop 2	.28	.34	.28	.34	.41	.38	.34	.36			.21
Lollipop 3	.30	.33	.39	.43	.55	.48	.59	.50			.31
Lollipop 4	.26	.27	.32	.33	.46	.44	.54	.36			.21
Achievement Test:											
KCAT			.35	.38	.37	.51	.52	.36			
Checklists:											
GKAP Readiness	.29										.17
GKAP Math											
CPR Readiness	.40	.46	.34	.31							.16
CPR Math	.33	.40	.32	.35							.21

p<.05 Bonferronni, N=858
All blank areas are non-significant.

TABLE 10

CANONICAL CORRELATIONS BETWEEN KINDERGARTEN PREDICTORS AND FIRST OR SECOND GRADE CRITERIA

	Grades						Test Scores				Retention in Kindergarten
Readiness Test:	Kindergarten		First		Second		First		Second		Kindergarten
							GA CRT		ITBS		
	Reading	Math	Reading	Math	Reading	Math	Reading	Math	Reading	Math	
Lollipop		.27		.25	.36	.21	.46	.26	.25	.22	.33
Achievement Test:											
KCAT			.35	.38	.37	.51	.52	.36			
Checklists:											
GKAP	.21		.17								.19
CPR		.30	.16	.17							.21

All blank areas are non-significant.

VALIDATION OF THE SPANISH LANGUAGE EDITION OF THE *LOLLIPOP TEST*

According to government projections, Hispanics are now the largest minority group in the United States. The need for a Hispanic edition of a culture-free school readiness test was a major motivation for the development of the Spanish language edition of the *Lollipop Test*. *La Prueba Lollipop: La Prueba Diagnostica y Seleccionadora de la Preparacion para la Escela-Enmendada* [*The Lollipop Test: A diagnostic Screening Test of School Readiness-Revised*] (Chew, 1989), was developed by complete translation of all components of the English version of the test, and field tested with bilingual Puerto Rican preschoolers. The Spanish translation was completed by Dr. Judith Schomber, Georgia Southern University. She also assisted with the on-site field testing in Puerto Rico. The translation of the 2007 edition of the Administration and Scoring Booklet was completed by M. Helena Hernandez, Assistant to the Dean of the College of Liberal Arts and Social Sciences, Georgia Southern University.

The Comparative Use of the Spanish and English Editions Of the *Lollipop Test*: A Cross Cultural Validation
(Lang, Chew, & Schomber, 1992)

Abstract

The object of this study was to compare the performance of similar preschool children on the Spanish and English versions of *The Lollipop Test: A Diagnostic Screening Test of School Readiness-Revised*. A stratified sample of three groups of preschoolers representing rural, disadvantaged, and bilingual children were administered the *Lollipop Test*. Discriminant analysis supported the conclusion that the *Lollipop Test* does not distinguish between similar students who have similar backgrounds and there is no evidence of bias in the Spanish form of the test. This is interpreted as support for the construct validity of the instrument.

The study was developed in the following manner:

Rationale

The need for an Hispanic edition of a culture-free school readiness test was the major motivation for the development of the Spanish language edition of the *Lollipop Test*.

The overriding objective of this research was to compare the performance of similar preschool children on the Spanish and English versions of the *Lollipop Test*. By using demographically parallel samples containing low income, but culturally different children, any pattern of systematic differences in the two versions of the test or cultural bias in the results should be statistically detectable. Additional motivation for the study is the idea that the Spanish edition of the *Lollipop Test* could be used as one component of a preschool or early school measurement battery, along with either the Spanish version of the *McCarthy Scales* or the *PPVT-R*, for accurate bilingual assessment.

Subjects

Subjects in this design consisted of three separate groups of preschool children. These groups were notably alike in major demographic characteristics (age and sex) of concern to the study yet differed in language and culture. Group 1 (Bilingual) contained 148 children registered in the Antilles School in Puerto Rico. The majority spoke Spanish as a first language and observed Puerto Rican cultural customs. Group II (Rural) contained 129 children enrolled in a primary school in southern Georgia. This primary school is located in a small community approximately one hundred miles from the nearest urban center. Group III (Disadvantaged) contained 788 children enrolled in Head Start programs throughout the state of Georgia. All three groups were approximately one half male (or female), and could generally be described as having a majority classified as low socioeconomic scale (welfare or labor). All three groups contained children who would be entering kindergarten and were approximately five years of age, with an average age of 62.03 months. The family income and parents' occupations were available for Groups I and II while Group III children must have met the Head Start guidelines as disadvantaged. A summary of the characteristics of the subjects is found in Table 11.

Procedures

Arrangements for testing incoming kindergarten students Group I: (bilingual) were made with the Antilles Elementary School in Puerto Rico. This school lies within the greater San Juan metropolitan area. About 80% of the students were transported by bus to the school.

Copies of the Spanish translation of the *Lollipop Test*--complete with the Spanish translations of the Developmental and Interpretive Manual for the *Lollipop Test* and Lollipop Stimulus Cards--were mailed to the school approximately one week prior to the testing, and inservice was provided to the staff members who were to conduct the assessment. The testing was completed during the first two weeks of August, 1989, as children were brought in by their parents to register. All the assessors were bilingual and were teachers from kindergarten or first grade.

In addition to the *Lollipop Test* scores, data was gathered on the socioeconomic level of each subject's family. The parents' occupations were available from school records. From this, family income was estimated and the students were summarized into four categories: welfare, labor, trade, and professional.

The test translator held a debriefing with each of the four examiners at the Antilles School to learn of any problems with the Spanish language translation. There were only a few concerns, all of which centered on regional interpretation of several vocabulary items. The administration manual was also critiqued by the Antilles School staff, and their suggestions for clarity were noted. No major changes were suggested, and all changes needed to clarify the administration and scoring were incorporated into the Spanish language version.

Group II (rural) data was collected as children were registered as part of the usual process for kindergarten admissions in rural, southern Georgia. The students were tested in May of 1985, and the assessors were trained examiners. Socioeconomic data was obtained anonymously through the school office and, again, was classified into categories. The sample consisted of 95 white and 34 African American children.

Group III (disadvantaged) data was collected from both urban and rural Georgia Head Start Center. The Head Start Centers compiled the data on score-report sheets and sent the scores to the researchers. Of the scores received, 788 had complete data and represented the age range pertinent to this study. The sample consisted of 284 white children, 490 African American children and 14 children of other minorities.

TABLE 11

DEMOGRAPHIC COMPARISON OF THE SAMPLES ON THREE DIFFERENT CULTURAL GROUPS

	Group I (Bilingual)	Group II (Rural)	Group III (Disadvantaged)
Number (N)	148	129	788
Sex (%)			
Male	48%	46%	48%
Female	52%	54%	52%
Age (μ in months)	61.9%	62.0	62.2
(σ)	3.7	3.8	3.9
Socioeconomic Scale (SES)			
Welfare (Below $10,000)	8.7%	17.8%	These students were screened as disadvantaged by the Head Start Program and were Typically from low income families. No specific data was available.
Labor ($10,000-$15,000)	53.3%	65.1%	
Trade ($15,000-$30,000)	21.6%	10.0%	
Professional (Above $30,000)	18.2%	6.9%	

Statistical Results and Discussion

Descriptive statistics were computed for all three groups for the four subtests of the *Lollipop Test*. No differences appeared that could be interpreted as indicating that the data came from different populations. The means, standard deviations and shapes of the score distributions were roughly similar. Even if "significant" statistical differences existed, examination reveals those differences would not be practical but were only due to the power of large samples. The results are summarized in Table 12.

All of the test characteristics differ by less than the probable differences that are due to sampling error. In fact, the slight differences that were found were less than the authors expected since the sample groups were only roughly matched by demographics that were expected to confound the results, not by a one-to-one matching design.

Additionally, the corollary of concluding that there are no differences between groups as demonstrated by the two versions of the test is that there is no evidence of systematic bias (lower scores) for the bilingual group. This suggests that the construction of the test, and the measurement of school readiness has not been confounded with culturally loaded items, a common problem with test translations. Additional statistical results can be found in the above cited reference.

TABLE 12

DESCRIPTIVE STATISTICS FOR *LOLLIPOP TEST* SCORES ON THREE DIFFRERENT CULTURAL GROUPS

	Group I (Bilingual) N = 148		Group II (Rural) N = 129		Group III (Disadvantaged) N = 788	
Means						
Subtest 1*	14.041		14.038		15.051	
Subtest 2	11.265		12.085		11.626	
Subtest 3	11.388		10.666		11.879	
Subtest 4	7.531		8.193		8.204	
Variance (Standard Deviation / Standard Error)						
Subtest 1*	2.8 /	.234	2.0 /	.262	2.6 /	.092
Subtest 2	3.5 /	.285	3.4 /	.302	3.5 /	.124
Subtest 3	5.2 /	.429	5.2 /	.459	4.8 /	.173
Subtest 4	6.3 /	1.183	6.8 /	.602	6.1 /	.216
Distribution (Skew / Kurtosis)						
Subtest 1*	-1.8 /	4.5	1.7 /	6.9	-1.9 /	4.3
Subtest 2	-.2 /	-.8	-.5 /	2.7	-.6 /	-.4
Subtest 3	-.5 /	-1.0	.2 /	1.5	.1 /	-.6
Subtest 4	.4 /	-1.3	.2 /	-1.5	.1 /	-1.4

*Subtest 1: Identification of Colors and Shapes
Subtest 2: Picture Description, Position, and Spatial Recognition
Subtest 3: Identification of Numbers and Counting
Subtest 4: Identification of Letters and Writing

Concurrent Validation and Regression Line Comparison of the *Lollipop Test* on a Bilingual Population

(Chew and Lang, 1993)

Abstract

The purpose of this study was to examine the concurrent validity of the Spanish edition of the *Lollipop Test* as an appropriate alternative preschool assessment instrument for bilingual Hispanic children using the *Developmental Indicators for the Assessment of Learning-Revised* (DIAL-R) as the criterion in a concurrent validity assessment. A strong multivariate relationship existed when preschoolers took one test, *La Prueba Lollipop*, in Spanish and another, the DIAL-R, in English ($r_{canonical} = .793$). These results support the concurrent validity of *La Prueba Lollipop* with bilingual Hispanic children. An additional analysis was made of the regression line comparison of the Spanish and English forms of *The Lollipop Test* using the DIAL as a criterion. No ethnic group bias was detected.

The study was conducted in the following manner:

Rationale

The practical purpose of this research was to examine the validity of the Spanish edition of the *Lollipop Test* as an appropriate alternative preschool assessment instrument for bilingual Hispanic children using the *Developmental Indicators for the Assessment of Learning-Revised* (DIAL-R) as the criterion in a concurrent validity assessment.

A corollary analysis of the concurrent validity assessment was the examination of the regression lines of the bilingual and English-speaking subjects for equivalence. *The Lollipop Test* was the predictor and the DIAL was the criterion for the regression.

Subjects

The sample of 148 bilingual children (71 males, 77 females) constituted the entire group of children being screened for admission to kindergarten (for the 1989 school year) at Antilles Elementary School in Puerto Rico. The majority of the students speak Spanish as a first language and observe Puerto Rican cultural customs. The mean chronological age at the time of testing was 61.9 months. The family incomes and parental occupations were made available through school records.

A second set of children were used as a comparison group for the regression line analysis. The data were collected as children were registered as part of the usual process for kindergarten admissions in rural, southern Georgia. The students were tested in May of 1985, and the assessors were trained examiners. This sample consisted of 95 white and 34 African American children. The mean chronological age at the time of testing was 62.0 months.

Procedures

During the first two weeks of August, 1989, each child in the bilingual sample was individually administered *La Prueba Lollipop* according to manual instructions by kindergarten or first-grade teachers who were bilingual. The children were randomly selected for testing as they were brought in by their parents to register for the 1989-90 kindergarten year.

The DIAL-R was also administered during August of 1989. The DIAL-R and its predecessor, the DIAL (Mardell and Goldenberg, 1975), is regularly used at the Antilles Elementary School. The staff was experienced in its use, and it provided an appropriate criterion for concurrent validity research. Though the DIAL-R was written in English, the examiners utilized Spanish translations whenever children experienced difficulty in understanding directions or terms.

The regression comparison scores were obtained from a sample regularly tested as part of normal preschool admissions in a rural American school in Georgia. The regression line generated from the scores obtained from these 129 English-speaking students was compared with the parallel line calculated for scores obtained from the Spanish-speaking children to detect differential slopes or intercepts as a result of systematic bias between the groups. In both cases, the DIAL served as the criterion.

Statistical Results and Discussion

Table 13 displays the bivariate (Pearson r) and multivariate (canonical r) correlation between subjects of both instruments. All correlations on coefficients were positive and statically significant at or beyond the .01 level. There was a strong multivariate relationship ($r_{canonical}$ = .79) between preschooler's scores on the *La Prueba Lollipop*, in Spanish, and the DIAL-R, in English. This underscores the principle that construct validity in early development should be culturally independent if the language barrier is overcome. The suggestion that *La Prueba Lollipop* be utilized as one component of a preschool measurement battery, along with either the Spanish version of the McCarthy Scales or the PPVT-R, might be considered as a viable alternative in the assessment of Hispanic children.

The regression lines for each pair of scores were examined across language using the Potthoff (1966) technique. No significant differences of slope, intercept, or residuals were found.

TABLE 13

BIVARIATE AND MULTIVARIATE RELATIONSHIPS BETWEEN THE SUBTESTS OF LA PRUEBA LOLLIPOP AND THE DIAL-R
(N = 148)

Subtest	Lollipop 1	Lollipop 2	Lollipop 3	Lollipop 4
DIAL-R 1: Motor	.61	.29	.46	.50
DIAL-R 2: Concepts	.66	.43	.65	.54
DIAL-R 3: Language	.51	.33	.34	.33

All $p < .01$.
$r_{canonical} = .793$; $X^2 = 157.05$, $p < .001$.

These results support the concurrent validity of *La Prueba Lollipop* with bilingual Hispanic children. In fact, the $r_{canonical} = .793$ is similar to that reported in a previous criterion-related study of the English version of the *Lollipop Test* and the DIAL where the multivariate relationship was reported as $r_{canonical} = .837$ (Chew and Lang, 1990).

VALIDATION OF THE FRENCH VERSION
OF THE *LOLLIPOP TEST*

The French translation of the *Lollipop Test* was developed by Dr. Sylvie Normandeau at the University of Montreal. Dr. Normandeau was given permission to translate and utilize the *Lollipop Test* with the understanding that she would disseminate results of her research efforts. In fact, Dr. Normandeau has shared some of her early research with Drs. Alex L. Chew and W. Steve Lang, including some French *Lollipop Test* scores. These students' scores were included in our study of multilingual testing with the *Lollipop Test,* which is reported on page 40 of this manual under the heading of "Trilingual Comparison of Translations of the *Lollipop Test.*"

The French translation of the *Lollipop Test* has been validated with a population of French-speaking preschoolers (Venet, Normandeau, Letarte, & Bigras, 2003). Children in the sample were longitudinally assessed four times with the *Lollipop Test* as well as two other cognitive assessment tools, the WPSSI-R and EVIP (which is the French version of PPVT-R), on the one hand, and twice with the PSA-A, which is the French version of SCBC-30, a tool designed to screen social and emotional problems in children aged 3 to 6 years, on the other hand. Furthermore, academic performance was assessed in a sub-sample at the end of their first school year. Correlation and regression analyses demonstrated convergent and divergent validity over the three years of the study. The French translation of the *Lollipop Test* demonstrated both internal consistency (Table 14) and test-retest reliability (Table 15) as a total test and by each of the four subtests.

TABLE 14

INTERNAL CONSISTENCY (CHRONBACH'S ALPHA) FOR THE FRENCH *LOLLIPOP TEST* FOR FOUR TESTINGS

Lollipop Test	Beginning Preschool (N = 274)	Ending Preschool (N = 258)	Beginning Kindergarten (N = 244)	Ending Kindergarten (N = 238)
Lollipop Total	0.89	0.89	0.88	0.84
Lollipop Subtest 1	0.69	0.66	0.65	0.40
Lollipop Subtest 2	0.50	0.55	0.43	0.19
Lollipop Subtest 3	0.87	0.87	0.86	0.83
Lollipop Subtest 4	0.77	0.79	0.80	0.87

TABLE 15

TEST-RETEST RELIABILITY FOR THE FRENCH *LOLLIPOP TEST* FOR FOUR TESTINGS

	N	Subtest 1	Subtest 2	Subtest 3	Subtest 4	Lollipop Total
Beginning Preschool To Ending Preschool	274	0.72	0.50	0.76	0.81	0.86
Beginning Preschool To Beginning Kindergarten	244	0.60	0.38	0.65	0.75	0.81
Beginning Preschool to Ending Kindergarten	258	0.48	0.12*	0.39	0.51	0.58
Beginning Kindergarten To Ending Kindergarten	238	0.50	0.39	0.65	0.63	0.70

All correlation coefficients significant at p < 0.001 except one indicated by asterisk.

A regression analysis was also completed to verify factors that predict school achievement at the end of first grade was calculated, with the following predictors entered in a first group of predictors: years of school completed by mother, years of school completed by father, family income, sex of child, pro-social behavior, anxious behavior, aggressive behavior, verbal ability, and WPPSI. The *Lollipop Test* administered in pre-kindergarten adds to the prediction of children's school achievement at the end of first grade (b = 0.32).

This group also assessed convergent validity and discriminant validity which presents correlations between the score on the *Lollipop Test* and measures of cognitive functioning (WWPSSI-R and EVIP [a measure of verbal ability]) and measures of prosocial, anxious or aggressive behavior (PSA). Correlations were calculated for children at the beginning of pre-kindergarten and at the beginning of kindergarten. Results indicate that children with higher scores on the *Lollipop Test* have higher scores on the WPPSI-R and the EVIP (they have better verbal abilities). Children with higher scores on the *Lollipop Test* are more prosocial, less anxious and less aggressive. In summary, the *Lollipop Test* proved to be reliable and stable over time, consistently correlated to other cognitive tests and predictive of academic performance assessed almost three years later. Since it is fast, easy to administer and score, the French *Lollipop Test* appears to be a very useful and reliable screening tool.

Table 16 is a norms table for the French translation of the *Lollipop Test*. This norms table was developed by the same group of researchers cited above in the French-Canadian validation study. The norms are based on a sample of 673 girls and 639 boys ranging in age from 53 to 67 months. As an example of how to utilize this table, consider a 6-year-old (72 months) girl who scored 65 on the *Lollipop Test*. Her score would place her at the 75th percentile rank. A boy of the same age, and achieving the same score, would fall at the 80th percentile rank.

TABLE 16

French *Lollipop Test* Norms

Girls: Percentile Rank

N	Age in Months	1	5	10	15	20	25	30	35	40	45	50	55	60	65	70	75	80	85	90	95	99	Mean	SD
102	53-58	2	15	18	19	22	24	25	26	27	29	30	32	34	37	38	39	42	44	49	51	55	31.5	11.7
100	59-63	9	20	24	27	31	35	37	38	39	40	41	42	43	46	49	50	53	55	57	60	64	41.4	13.6
232	64-70	17	26	31	37	40	42	44	45	47	48	49	51	52	53	55	57	58	61	63	65	67	48.4	11.4
239	71-76	36	47	50	53	54	56	57	59	60	61	62	63			64	65		66	67	68	69	60.0	6.9

N = 673

Boys : Percentile Rank

N	Age in Months	1	5	10	15	20	25	30	35	40	45	50	55	60	65	70	75	80	85	90	95	99	Mean	SD
116	53-58	7	10	15	19	21	22	23	24	26	28	29	31	34	35	37	40	43	47	51	60	63	31.7	13.6
115	59-63	11	17	25	26	27	29	32	36	38	40	41	44	46	47	50	52	54	56	60	63	67	41.0	14
198	64-70	20	26	32	37	39	42	43	45	48	49	51	52	53	54	56	57	59	62	63	65	67	49.0	11.6
210	71-76	30	43	48	51	53	54	56	57	58	59	60	61	62	63		64	65	66	67	68	69	58.5	8.0

N = 639
Total N = 1312

39

INTERPRETATION OF *LOLLIPOP TEST* SCORES BY LANGUAGE AND ETHNICITY

Sometimes, students enter a program at approximately four years old as representative of multicultural/multilingual groups. The students, after a year or more of immersion and instruction in English, may be capable of being tested in English. Unfortunately, some have little experience with English or use a mixture of French/English or Spanish/English to communicate. The *Lollipop Test* has been translated into French and Spanish and used as an instrument or criterion in several research studies conducted outside the United States. The Spanish version, *La Prueba Lollipop*, is currently available. The Spanish translation was completed by Dr. Judith Schomber at Georgia Southern University. The French translation was developed at the University of Montreal by Dr. Sylvie Normandeau. Dr. Normandeau's validation of the *Lollipop Test* is reported in a published paper in French (Venet, Normandeau, Letarte, & Bigras, 2003). The *Lollipop Test* has been utilized in an on-going French-Canadian longitudinal study (Centre of Excellence for Early Childhood Development, April, 2006).

In some cases where gain scores are desired and the students are instructed in English; a pre-post design may use a non-English version for the pretest and the English version as the posttest. If the students are instructed in native French and Spanish, they may be tested both times in the native language. Because of the language mix and the common finding of lower SES of these students, gains from 8 to 15 points is typical, but slightly less with non-LEP (Limited English Proficiency) students.

Regardless, the means and standard deviations shown in Table 17, appear to be equivalent across forms and for different demographic groups. An initial study using the Rasch model of item response theory concluded that the Spanish and English versions produced similar fit statistics for most items on a small sample (Lang, Chew, & Vargas, 1993, 1995). For interested researchers, an upcoming analysis with item response theory with details of multilingual testing with the *Lollipop Test* is scheduled for the American Educational Research Association Conference in 2007. Please contact Drs. Alex L. Chew or Steve Lang for the final results of this study and the most current analyses.

TABLE 17

TRILINGUAL COMPARISON OF TRANSLATIONS OF THE *LOLLIPOP TEST*

Group Demographics	Entry Mean	Entry SD	Entry N	Exit Mean	Exit SD	Exit N	Change** Mean	Change** SD
English	31.1	14.2	199	55.4	10.6	104	24	2
French	32.2	12.6	229	40.9	13.2	234	8	0.5
Spanish	32.5	16.0	42	48.4	12.4	68	14	1
Male	30.5	13.0	222	45.2	13.7	209	15	1
Female	33.0	14.1	247	49.6	14.4	225	16	1
White	32.9	13.1	297	45.2	13.9	303	13	1
Hispanic	29.9	14.0	107	54.1	12.5	66	14	1
Black	29.9	14.1	48	53.3	12.7	48	13	1
Other*	29.8	15.6	18	46.1	16.5	18	16	1
Total	31.8	14.2	470	54.1	12.5	66	13	1

*Students identified as mixed, Eastern, or Native American.
**Traditional vs. LEP and subgroup expectations for a year of instruction in English in rounded figures.

Trilingual Sample

For the most part, the data in the above table are for the same students both pre- and post-tested. A few students in this sample left a program or entered during the middle of the year so the number of students entering does not always equal the number present at the end of the year. Data were collected from multiple states in the US and provinces in Canada. Students were typically administered the *Lollipop Test* in their native language, but some were "mixed-up lingual" with no clear language established at such a young age.

Programs differed widely as to the length of day, teacher quality, and class size. Obviously, some programs test on entry in a native language, but the program intent was to teach English, so they would usually not post-test in a native language. Regardless of language, the evidence supports equivalence of the tests. Gain scores across languages is confounded by numerous variables such as language of instruction, type of program, late entries, and attrition.

Some students came from pre-kindergarten or Head Start programs with an age range from 48 months to 60 months. Others were enrolled in a kindergarten program for 5-year-olds, but some programs were half-day and others were full-day.

Program Gain Expectation Recommendation

A rule of thumb based on means for targeting is that students would gain about ½ SD or 7-8 points as a beginning 4 year old in a pre-kindergarten program and 1 SD or 15 points in a traditional 5 year old beginning kindergarten though this varies by individual and type of program.

Research Conclusions

1. The *Lollipop Test* appears to be equivalent across the languages tested.
2. The *Lollipop Test* appears to be gender and ethnically fair.
3. The *Lollipop Test* appears to be useful to show gains for pre-kindergarten, Head Start, and kindergarten programs.

INTERPRETATION AND UTILIZATION OF SCORES

National norms, as such, have not been established for the *Lollipop Test*. However, some system-wide norms, and specialty norms, e.g. Georgia Head Start Programs, have been developed. These are presented in later sections of this manual as "Examples of Norms Tables." Also, descriptive statistics were computed for the validation studies mentioned previously in this manual. These are presented in Tables 18 and 19. Although this data may not represent typical performance of students in other school systems or pre-school programs, a comparison of scores with the results of these studies may be helpful in some instances.

Descriptive Statistics for Validation Studies of the *Lollipop Test*

TABLE 18

VALIDATION OF THE *LOLLIPOP TEST*
(Chew & Morris, 1984)

| | Lollipop Test Subtests | | | | |
	Lollipop 1	Lollipop 2	Lollipop 3	Lollipop 4	Lollipop Test Total
Mean	15.41	14.12	15.14	15.49	60.16
Median	16.00	15.00	17.00	18.00	63.00
Mode	17.00	17.00	17.00	18.00	67.00
Range	14.00	12.00	15.00	18.00	58.00
Standard Error	.11	.16	.18	.23	.55
Standard Deviation	1.85	2.74	3.03	3.89	9.35

N = 293

Utilizing the statistics contained in Table 18, suggested readiness score ranges are as follows:

Suggested Score Ranges for End of Kindergarten Administration:

65 & Above - **Above Average** Readiness

62 – 64   - High Average Readiness

59 – 61   - Average Readiness

56 - 58   - Low Average Readiness

55 & Below - **Below Average** Readiness

Note: These scores were made by kindergarten students during the first two weeks of May, with a mean of 8.6 months enrolled in kindergarten. Mean age at time of testing was 74.4 months.

TABLE 19

VALIDATION OF THE *LOLLIPOP TEST* AS A
PRE-KINDERGARTEN SCREENING INSTRUMENT
(Chew & Morris, 1987)

| | Lollipop Test Subtests | | | | |
	Lollipop 1	Lollipop 2	Lollipop 3	Lollipop 4	Lollipop Test Total
Mean	14.04	12.09	10.67	8.19	44.98
Median	14.70	12.58	10.63	7.69	44.88
Mode	17.00	13.00	17.00	8.00	43.00
Range	17.00	16.00	17.00	18.00	68.00
Standard Error	.27	.30	.46	.60	1.37
Standard Deviation	3.04	3.43	5.22	6.84	15.51

N = 129

Utilizing the statistics contained in Table 19, suggested readiness score ranges are as follows:

Suggested Score Ranges for Pre-Kindergarten Administration:

54 & Above - **Above Average** Readiness

48 – 53   - High Average Readiness

43 – 47   - Average Readiness

37 - 42   - Low Average Readiness

36 & Below - **Below Average** Readiness

Note: These scores were made by pre-kindergarten subjects during the second week of May, prior to entering kindergarten the following fall. Mean age at time of testing was 62.1 months.

An individual's score on the *Lollipop Test* is best interpreted in terms of measures of central tendency of the group of which he or she was a member when tested. Also of considerable significance is the time or date of testing, i.e., pre-kindergarten, post-kindergarten, or beginning first grade. When interpreting scores to teachers and parents, it is sometimes helpful to develop a simple frequency distribution chart for use as a visual aid. Such a chart facilitates the graphic presentation of an individual's score, as compared to the group or class as a whole.

Table 20 is an example of a frequency distribution chart range for pre-kindergarten students. Also, examining the measures of central tendency for the group based on the data from the study validating the *Lollipop Test* as a pre-kindergarten screening instrument (Chew & Morris, 1987). Examining this frequency chart on the following page, the reader can see that a score of 52 was made by 1 student, and if you look at the suggested score ranges following Table 19, it is within the high average readiness (Table 19), you can see that the individual's score of 52 is approximately one-half standard deviation above the mean of 44.98. The cumulative percentage of 67 suggests that the score of 52 was as high or higher than 67 percent of the scores made by other members of the group.

TABLE 20

FREQUENCY DISTRIBUTION OF SCORES OBTAINED ON THE *LOLLIPOP TEST* BY PRE-KINDERGARTEN SUBJECTS

Score Obtained	Frequency	Cumulative Percent	Score Obtained	Frequency	Cumulative Percent
1	1	1	43	6	47
13	1	2	44	3	49
16	2	3	45	4	52
18	2	3	46	5	56
19	1	5	47	5	60
20	2	6	48	1	60
21	1	7	49	2	62
22	1	8	50	4	65
23	1	9	51	1	66
24	1	9	52	1	67
25	4	12	53	1	67
26	2	14	54	1	68
27	3	16	55	2	70
29	1	17	57	2	71
30	3	19	58	3	74
31	2	21	59	1	74
32	4	24	60	1	75
33	3	26	61	4	78
34	2	28	62	3	81
35	3	30	63	4	84
36	1	31	64	5	88
37	1	32	65	4	91
38	3	34	66	2	92
39	2	36	67	3	95
40	3	38	68	2	96
41	3	40	69	5	100
42	2	42			

N = 129

As discussed above, when utilizing and interpreting scores the *Lollipop Test*, it would be desirable to compute measures of central tendency and a frequency distribution for your group of students. The group may be as small as a single kindergarten class of 18 to 20 students; all the kindergarten classes in a school; or perhaps all the kindergarten classes in the school system, as presented in Table 20. However, such information would allow the description of a student's standing with respect to his individual class, his school or the system as a whole.

School systems desiring to utilize norms instead of the suggested criterion-referenced approach to interpretation of scores, may wish to collect data and establish their own local norms. The procedure for establishing local norms is discussed in the following section of this manual. Actually, there is much evidence in the current literature to suggest that local norms have considerably more value than national norms in assessment procedures with the new emphasis on, and trend toward, competency based educational programs.

The *Administration and Scoring Booklet for the Lollipop Test* provides an easy, convenient way to analyze each examinee's response to each specifiable and teachable task/skill--a competency-based, criterion-referenced approach. The teacher may wish to make a list of those items passed, and not passed, for each subtest. Should a child demonstrate a deficit on any area of the test, the teacher and/or instructional team planning his educational program can easily plan remedial strategies. When a child achieves a below average readiness score, he/she should be referred for additional psycho-educational assessment.

The *Lollipop Test* should be utilized primarily as a screening test to identify the child's deficits (and strengths) in readiness skills and to identify those children who may require additional psycho-educational evaluation. The author does not see the *Lollipop Test* as being used for excluding or postponing admission to school, but as an aid in developing the most appropriate program for each child's individual needs.

The literature reveals that there is little or no advantage to delayed or postponed admission to school for immature children. Kulberg & Gershman (1973) report initial findings in an on-going study of school readiness which has spanned four years. This study compared 5-year-olds in three types of school programs: (1) delayed admission, (2) experimental readiness class, and (3) traditional kindergarten. In the follow-up study, no differences were found in general achievement on the criterion measure at the end of the first year of school, even though children in the delayed admission group were a year older than the others.

The implication of these findings for educational programming and readiness assessment are interesting. Three groups of immature children arrive at the same point, as measured by test scores, as a result of three different kinds of programming. One group takes an additional year to get here. The one thing in common to all groups is a year of schooling, whether in kindergarten or readiness class. One might conclude tentatively that the year of schooling was the effective agent in producing the obtained level of achievement. Additionally, one might also suspect that readiness is amenable to and dependent upon environmental circumstances.

Somewhat similar findings were produced in an extensive research project conducted over four decades ago by Nimnich, Sparks & Mortensen (1963), which eventually involved more than 9,000 students in eighty-four Colorado school districts. The study was attempting to find the answer to the question: "Is there a right admission age?" Their findings suggested that the variable most commonly used--age--the least reliable predictor of school success.

EXAMPLES OF NORMS TABLES

Lollipop Test Norms for Head Start
Children in Georgia

The *Lollipop Test* has seen wide acceptance and utilization by Head Start programs throughout the United States. As a result of its popularity in Georgia, the *Lollipop Test Norms-Technical Manual for Head Start children in Georgia* (Lang and Chew, 1989a) was developed as an aid for the state's programs. The process of developing the technical manual and Georgia Head Start norms was presented at the annual meeting of the Georgia Education Research Association in Atlanta (Lang and Chew, 1989b). The manual was demonstrated to program coordinators at the Georgia Head Start Conference in Macon (Lang and Chew, 1990). Most of the coordinators in attendance had contributed to the normative data base. The Georgia Head Start norms tables were also shared at the 2001 Regional V Head Start Association Conference in Indianapolis (Chew, 2001).

The Norming Sample

The statistics in these norms tables were taken from a sample of 788 students whose complete Lollipop Test scores were available. Scores from partial or incomplete test results were excluded from this sample. The sample ranged from approximately four and one-half years to almost six years of age. All subjects were currently enrolled in a Head Start program in Georgia and represented a wide range of geographic districts. The demographics are described below.

Characteristics of the Sample

		Race			
		White	*Black*		
Sex	*Male*	135	247	382	(48.48%)
	Female	154	252	406	(51.52%)
		289	499	788	
		(36.67%)	(63.32%)		

Location of Schools in the Sample

	Urban	Rural	Mix of Urban & Rural
National Head Start	37%	31%	30%
Georgia Norming Sample	42%	31%	27%

47

The Explanation of the Norms Tables

Table 21 translates total scores obtained into percentile ranks and standard scores. **Percentile rank** is used to illustrate the percentage of students who would fall below the score in question. <u>Example</u>. The percentile rank associated with the score 55 is 66.3. This means that approximately 66% of the Head Start children used in this sample scored lower than 55. Percentile rank is useful to compare an individual student to the comparison group of their peers at a specific time. Percentile rank is NOT useful for aggregating scores (such as a school average) or computing progress from gain scores.

Standard scores are used to make comparisons across different tests. The column labeled "standard scores" on Table 21 has a mean of 100 and a standard deviation of 15. If you can identify the standard score used by other tests, comparisons might be made to the *Lollipop Test* for an individual student's profile on multiple measures. <u>Example</u>. An IQ score of 89 on the Peabody Picture Vocabulary Test (with its mean of 100 and a standard deviation of 15) is barely different than the Lollipop standard score of 91. Standard scores are also useful for research, group scores (such as a school average), or gain scores.

Table 22 lists **percentile rank by age** for Head Start children in Georgia. This table gives the percentile rank based on the age of the children who obtained a particular *Lollipop Test* Total score. <u>Example</u>. A child, aged four years and 10 months, who scored 55 on the *Lollipop Test* would achieve as 83rd percentile rank. This could be interpreted as doing better than 83 percent of the Head Start children his age included in this sample. When developing test norms, sometimes it is necessary to **interpolate** when an actual score is not achieved by the sample being tested. Therefore on Table 22, these interpolations or statistical estimates are denoted by the grey bars. This is a long time common practice among test developers and publishers.

A Word of Caution

Although Georgia and national Head Start demographics are similar, caution should be exercised when comparing Head Start students in your locale to this sample. It is possible that the percentile ranks and standard scores reported here are influenced by local factors such as the birth date required for school entry, length of the instructional day, class size, teacher qualifications, or adopted curriculum. Again, as previously suggested in this manual, the best approach to understanding your students' progress would be to establish local norms appropriate for your program. However, a comparison of your students with the Georgia Head Start norms could prove to be useful and convenient beginning strategy.

TABLE 21

STANDARD SCORES AND PERCENTILE RANK
FOR HEAD START CHILDREN IN GEORGIA

Total Score	Percentile Rank	Standard Score		Total Score	Percentile Rank	Standard Score
12	1.0	52.0		41	35.3	94.1
13	1.2	59.4		42	37.0	95.1
14	1.3	66.9		43	38.8	96.2
15	1.5	67.9		44	40.5	97.2
16	1.8	67.9		45	42.3	98.2
17	2.2	68.9		46	44.5	99.2
18	2.7	69.9		47	47.3	100.2
19	3.6	70.9		48	50.2	101.2
20	4.3	72.0		49	52.7	102.2
21	4.4	73.0		50	54.8	103.2
22	4.7	75.0		51	56.8	104.2
23	5.3	76.0		52	59.1	105.2
24	6.6	77.0		53	61.4	106.2
25	8.0	78.0		54	63.8	107.3
26	8.8	79.0		55	66.3	108.3
27	10.0	80.0		56	68.7	109.3
28	11.2	81.0		57	70.9	110.3
29	12.1	82.0		58	73.1	111.3
30	13.5	83.0		59	75.4	112.3
31	14.9	84.0		60	78.2	113.3
32	16.6	85.0		61	81.0	114.3
33	18.2	86.0		63	83.5	115.3
34	19.5	87.0		64	85.6	116.3
35	21.7	88.0		65	87.5	117.4
36	24.2	89.1		66	90.6	118.4
37	26.3	90.1		67	93.8	119.4
38	28.8	91.1		68	97.5	120.4
39	30.8	92.1		69	98.9	122.2
40	32.9	93.1				

N = 788

49

TABLE 22

PERCENTILE RANK BY AGE FOR HEAD START CHILDREN IN GEORGIA

AGE: YEARS – MONTHS

Total Score	4-8	4-9	4-10	4-11	5-0	5-1	5-2	5-3	5-4	5-5	5-6	5-7	5-8
10	---	---	---	---	---	---	---	---	---	---	---	---	---
15	3	4	2	3	2	1	6	3	2	2	3	1	2
16-17	6	5	4	5	2	1	6	3	2	2	4	1	2
18-19	9	6	6	6	2	2	6	4	3	3	4	2	3
20	12	7	8	8	2	2	6	4	3	3	5	2	3
21-22	13	10	11	9	3	3	7	5	3	4	5	2	3
22-23	14	12	15	10	4	4	8	7	4	6	6	3	3
25	15	15	18	11	5	5	9	8	4	7	6	3	3
26-27	18	20	24	13	8	7	10	10	5	8	7	5	5
28-29	21	25	29	16	10	8	10	12	5	10	7	7	6
30	24	30	35	18	13	10	11	14	6	11	8	9	8
31-32	27	33	39	21	16	14	12	18	7	12	9	11	9
33-34	29	36	43	25	18	19	14	22	8	12	11	12	10
35	32	39	47	28	21	23	15	26	9	13	12	14	11
36-37	35	44	50	33	25	29	17	29	14	16	15	16	16
38-39	37	48	53	39	29	35	20	33	18	18	17	19	21
40	40	53	56	44	33	41	22	36	23	21	20	21	26
41-42	43	55	59	47	36	45	26	38	29	25	23	24	29
43-44	47	56	61	50	38	49	29	41	34	29	25	28	33
45	50	58	64	53	41	53	33	43	40	33	28	31	36
46-47	56	61	66	57	44	56	38	48	45	37	33	36	42
48-49	62	65	69	60	48	60	43	52	50	41	38	41	48
50	68	68	71	64	51	63	48	57	55	45	43	46	54
51-52	69	70	75	68	56	66	52	61	61	49	45	50	58
53-54	69	72	79	71	62	69	57	66	67	52	48	54	63
55	70	74	83	75	67	72	61	70	73	56	50	58	67
56-57	76	78	87	78	70	75	65	75	78	59	54	63	70
58-59	81	81	90	80	73	78	70	81	82	63	58	68	74
60	87	85	94	83	76	81	74	86	87	66	62	73	77
61-62	90	89	94	88	80	85	80	90	91	72	68	77	83
63-64	93	92	95	93	85	89	85	95	94	77	74	80	90
65	96	96	95	98	89	93	91	99	98	83	80	84	96
69	---	---	---	---	---	---	---	---	---	---	---	---	---

The white bars are computed from sample data. The grey bars are estimates. N=788.

RE-TEST/PROGRAM ENTRY NORMS TABLES

In some cases, a district may desire to compare the entry scores of students of different ages, but who have never participated in a pre-school, pre-kindergarten, Head Start or similar program. Although sometimes older than typical, these beginning students might be appropriately compared with other beginners. Sometimes it might be helpful to a school system to know what can be expected for pre-test scores on the *Lollipop Test* depending on the entry age of the child.

This large sample was collected in Florida and Georgia from multiple school districts. The sample includes mostly PRETEST DATA (plus a few late entries) where the student has yet to attend preschool, kindergarten, or a Head Start program. The average age expected to enter kindergarten would be approximately 60 months or 5-years-old. This data starts with the 4 year old preschool program (48 months) and includes data from students late to enter school or repeating kindergarten at 6 years old (72 months).

The characteristics of the sample are shown below:

Male	Female	Total
449	479	928
48.3%	51.6%	100%

Black	White	Other	Total
316	455	157	928
34.0%	49.0%	16.9%	100%

"Expected" performance based on age, is given for *Lollipop Test* subtests and total score in Table 23. This table is intended to sample typical scores for the subtests of the *Lollipop Test* at different ages as they enter a variety of programs intended to precede first grade.

TABLE 23

EXPECTED NORMS BY LOLLIPOP TEST SUBTESTS AND TOTAL ON PRE-TEST SCORES FOR PROGRAM ENTRY

Age in Months	Lollipop Subtest 1 Mean	Lollipop Subtest 2 Mean	Lollipop Subtest 3 Mean	Lollipop Subtest 4 Mean	Total Test Mean	Number
48-50	8.1	7.2	5.2	2.4	22.8	37
51-53	8.4	8.3	7.8	4.4	28.9	53
54-56	10.3	8.7	9.3	6.5	34.8	79
57-59	12.2	9.6	10.4	8.9	41.4	199
60-62	12.6	10.5	10.9	9.7	43.8	149
63-65	13.5	10.9	11.4	9.9	45.9	173
66-68	14.3	11.3	13.2	10.8	49.6	163
69-71	14.5	12.4	13.4	11.0	50.6	40
72-74	14.8	12.8	13.7	13.7	53.0	65
Maximum Score	*17*	*17*	*17*	*18*	*69*	*958**

*The total sample was 958 students. Because gender or race was not reported for 30 students, the sample characteristics shown on the preceding page report 928 students.

LOCAL DISTRIBUTIONAL EVIDENCE OF PROGRAM IMPACT

It is common in educational setting today to seek evaluative evidence of program effectiveness. Because each school system and program has an individual setting, national norms may not be valid or apply to every situation. As such, it is often appropriate for a program to aggregate data for its own use. Here is an example of real data collected in 2005, but the district and its location are not provided.

Situation

In this case, a new preschool program desired an assessment of effectiveness. The students involved represented a very diverse population and evidence of fairness in testing would be appropriate. A corollary would be a future expectation of goals or targeted expectations of average gains of students. Below are some typical results that a program might consider.

Was the kindergarten program effective?

Two hundred students located at 16 elementary school kindergarten programs in the district were pre-tested and post-tested during one year on the *The Lollipop Test: A Diagnostic Screening Test of School Readiness*. Here is a summary of the results:

	Mean Score	SD	N
Pretest	31.3	14.2	199*
Posttest	55.4	10.6	200

* One child did not answer during the pretest.

Since the Lollipop Manual suggests that 31.3 is *below readiness* for first grade while 55.4 is *low average readiness*, and taking into account the diversity and large incidence of LEP students in the program: a conclusion that the program was effective at moving the students to *readiness* is appropriate.

Was the testing and program fair to all students?

Ethnic Identity	Pretest Mean	Posttest Mean	Gain	N
White	34.5	57.0	22.5	74
Hispanic	28.2	54.9	26.7	65
Black	30.4	54.3	23.9	47
Other*	31.1	52.7	21.6	13

*Students identified as mixed, Eastern, or Native American

Gender	Pretest Mean	Posttest Mean	Gain	N
Male	29.1	53.6	24.5	84
Female	32.8	56.7	23.9	115

Since the Lollipop Manual suggests that gains of 1 SD or 15 points per year is an appropriate goal for a program, this program appears to have exceeded that target. None of the subgroups appear to be substantially different in achievement despite the diversity, so the program appears to be working effectively with identified groups.

What can I do to help interpret the data for parents and teachers?

In Table 24 are local percentile rank tables for the local program data. With this information, you could talk with parents about the pre-test and post-test comparison of an individual student to the peer group. These ranks are appropriate for an individual student's scores. They are NOT appropriate for group interpretation.

TABLE 24

LOCAL PROGRAM PERCENTILE RANKS

PRE-KINDERGARTEN TEST SCORES

RAW SCORE	PERCENTILE RANK	RAW SCORE	PERCENTILE RANK
5	1	38	70
6	1	39	72
7	1	40	73
8	1	41	73
9	1	42	75
10	2	43	77
11	3	44	78
12	4	45	80
13	6	46	80
14	7	47	81
15	9	48	82
16	12	49	84
17	14	50	87
18	18	51	88
19	22	52	89
20	26	53	90
21	29	54	91
22	31	55	91
23	34	56	93
24	39	57	94
25	42	58	95
26	45	59	96
27	48	60	96
28	51	61	97
29	52	62	98
30	54	63	98
31	56	64	99
32	59	65	99
33	62	66	99
34	63	67	99
35	66	68	99
36	67	69	99
37	69		

N = 199

TABLE 24, Continued

LOCAL PROGRAM PERCENTILE RANKS

POST-KINDERGARTEN TEST SCORE

RAW SCORE	PERCENTILE RANK	RAW SCORE	PERCENTILE RANK
20	1	45	18
21	1	46	19
22	1	47	20
23	1	48	22
24	1	49	24
25	1	50	25
26	1	51	28
27	1	52	30
28	1	53	32
29	2	54	35
30	2	55	38
31	3	56	41
32	4	57	45
33	4	58	47
34	5	59	50
35	5	60	55
36	6	61	60
37	7	62	65
38	9	63	71
39	11	64	78
40	12	65	85
41	13	66	88
42	14	67	93
43	16	68	97
44	18	69	99

N = 200

DEVELOPING LOCAL NORMS FOR THE *LOLLIPOP TEST*

Utilizing Local Norms

Local norms are sometimes better and more appropriate than national norms. However, if local norms are based on a group of adequate size (usually 200 or more students), they can be used in most of the ways that national norms are used. Some possible uses of local norms include: (1) describing a student's standing with respect to the local group, (2) comparing the scores of two local students, (3) comparing a student's standing with his school and/or system standing, and (4) in the case of the *Lollipop Test* comparing a student's scores with others who have made similar scores and have or have not been successful in first grade academic work.

The reader who is planning on developing local norms for the *Lollipop Test* would find it helpful to consult several sources of educational and psychological measurement and evaluation. For example, Gronlund & Linn (1990) and Anastasi (1988) have excellent chapters on norms. An additional source on basic statistical concepts would also be helpful.

Collecting Data for Local Norms

As previously mentioned, scores for 200 or more students are usually desirable for constructing local norms. Percentile ranks can be computed for a smaller group of students, but the larger the group the more stable the norms will be. The Educational Testing Service (ETS) (1964) points out that the norms do not have to come from the same testing period and can be accumulated over a period of several years. The scores used, however, should all be obtained on comparable groups of students at comparable stages in their schooling. For example, you may wish to test students with the *Lollipop Test* after they complete eight months in kindergarten or during the first two weeks of the first grade. In either case, you would need a separate set of data, one for students completing kindergarten and one for entering first grades.

For those schools or school systems collecting data over several years it is recommended that they drop the oldest data from their local norms and add the newest data periodically. Systems doing this, may also want to keep a running record of the mean and variance of local norms as described by Elliot & Bretzing (1980), and if using a computer, by Krus & Ceurvorst (1978).

Making a Grouped Frequency Distribution

After acquiring a pool of test data, the initial step in constructing local norms is to prepare a frequency distribution. The procedure, as suggested by Chew (1984), is outlined below using mock *Lollipop Test* scores from a May, 2006 administration in Any County School System's ten kindergarten classes as an example:

1) Find the highest score and lowest score.

2) Set up two-score intervals running from the highest score down to the lowest and including both: e.g., 68-69, 66-67, 64-64, etc. (See Table 25 on next page.) Notice that each interval begins with an even number. Also, note that no score intervals overlap; for example, if the two intervals 68-69 and 67-68 were listed, you would not know where to put a score of 68.

TABLE 25

LOCAL NORMS SCORES DISTRIBUTION SHEET

Name of Test: **The *Lollipop Test***   Date(s) of Testing: **May, 2018**

School(s) or System: **Any County School System**   Grade or Class: **Kindergarten Class**

Selected Characteristics
of Local Norms Group: **104 boys; 114 girls; mean months in kindergarten – 8.12**

Score Interval	Tally					Frequency	Cumulative Frequency	Percentile Rank
68-69	IIIII	IIIII	II			12	218	97
66-67	IIIII	IIIII				10	206	92
64-65	IIIII	IIIII	IIII			14	196	87
62-63	IIIII	IIIII	II			12	182	81
60-61	IIIII	IIIII	IIIII	IIIII	IIII	24	170	72
58-59	IIIII	IIIII	IIIII	IIIII		20	146	62
56-57	IIIII	IIIII	IIIII			15	126	54
54-55	IIIII	IIIII	IIIII			15	111	47
52-53	IIIII	IIIII	II			12	96	41
50-51	IIIII	IIIII	II			12	84	36
48-49	IIIII	IIII				9	72	31
46-47	IIIII	IIIII				10	63	27
44-45	IIIII	III				8	53	22
42-43	IIIII	III				8	45	19
40-41	IIIII					5	37	16
38-39	IIII					4	32	14
36-37	II					2	28	12
34-35	IIIII	I				6	26	11
32-33	IIIII	I				6	20	8
30-31	II					2	14	6
28-29	IIIII	I				6	12	4
26-27	IIIII	I				6	6	1

Total Number of Students: **218**

58

3) List the score intervals from the highest to the lowest on a sheet of lined paper, such as a legal pad. (See example in the first column of the table on the preceding page.)

4) Tally the number of students earning scores falling in each interval. (See table, second column.)

5) Sum the tallies in each score interval and record these frequencies in the third column, which is headed "Frequency."

Computing Percentile Ranks

Cumulative frequencies are obtained by adding frequencies in the score distributed from the bottom up. The number opposite each score interval equals the sum of the frequency for that interval and all frequencies below it. (See table, fourth column.) Percentile ranks for any score interval are computed from these cumulative frequencies in the following manner:

1) Find one half the frequency for a particular score interval,

2) Add the result of (1) to the cumulative frequency for the score interval just below the interval being computed.

3) Divide the result of (2) by the total number of students in the norms group, and

4) Multiply the answer from (3) by 100.

From the 60-61 score interval in the table, the following computations were made:

1) ½ x 24 = 12

2) 12 + 146 = 158

3) 158 ÷ 218 = .72 (taking the answer to the nearest hundredth)

4) .72 x 100 = 72

The percentile rank of 72 is recorded in the fifth column of the table.

According to ETS (1964), percentile ranks computed in this manner are mid-percentile ranks, i.e., they correspond to the midpoint of the two-score interval and apply approximately to both scores in the interval.

In the computation of local norms utilizing larger score intervals, the following formula may be helpful:

$$PR = 100 \left[\frac{(\text{Raw score} - \text{LRL of class})}{i} \times (f \text{ of the class}) + (\text{cum. } f \text{ of the interval}) \div N \right]$$

Symbols: PR = Percentile Rank
            LRL = Lower Real Limits
              i = Number of units contained in the score interval
              f = Frequency
              N = Sum of the Frequencies (total cases)

Interpretation of Local Percentile Norms

Percentile rank is a statement of a person's relative position within a defined group. Therefore, a percentile rank of 72 indicates a score that is as high as or higher than those made by 72 percent of the people in that particular group.

Many test publishers, as well as developers of local norms, have found it useful to prepare norms tables in the form of percentile bands. The objective in using percentile bands is to keep the test user from attaching unwarranted precision to a test score. The band that is usually reported extends one standard error of measurement on either side of the obtained score. The reader, who is interested in setting up percentile bands for local norms on the *Lollipop Test,* should consult any elementary or basic text on statistics in education and psychology for suggested procedures.

CHRONOLOGICAL SUMMARY OF
LOLLIPOP TEST RESEARCH

AUTHOR(S)	DATE	SIGNIFICANCE OF STUDY	MEDIA
Chew	1977	Construct Validation & Factor Analysis	Dissertation
Chew	1981	*Lollipop Test* Initially Published	Publication
Chew	1983	Concurrent Validity	Paper Presentation
Chew & Morris	1984	Concurrent Validity	Journal Article
Chew, Kesler, & Sudduth	1984	Developing Local Norms	Journal Article
Chew	1985	Pre-Kindergarten Screening	Paper Presentation
Chew & Morris	1987	Pre-Kindergarten Screening	Journal Article
Chew & Morris	1989	Predictive Validity	Journal Article
Chew	1989	*Lollipop Test, Revised*	Publication
Chew	1989	Spanish Edition Published	Administration & Scoring Booklet Published
Lang & Chew	1989	Development of Head Start Norms	Paper Presentation
Lang & Chew	1989	Norms Technical Manual for Head Start Children in Georgia	Non-Published Manual
Chew & Lang	1990	Predictive Validity	Journal Article
Lang & Chew	1990	Utilizing *Lollipop Test* Norms	Paper Presentation
Lang, Chew, & Schomber	1990	Construct Validity of Spanish Edition	Paper Presentation

Chew & Lang	1992	Predictive Validity of Spanish Edition	Journal Article
Lang, Chew, & Schomber	1992	Equating Spanish & English Editions (Fairness) by Regression	Journal Article
Chew & Lang	1993	Concurrent Validity of Spanish Edition	Journal Article
Lang, Chew & Vargas	1993	Application Analysis (Rasch Model) & Comparison of Spanish & English Editions	Paper Presentation
Vargas & Lang	1994	Cultural Fairness of the Spanish & English Editions (Rasch Model)	Journal Article
Lang, Chew, & Vargas	1995	Equating the Spanish & English Editions (Rasch Model)	Paper Presentation & ERIC Article
Lang, Chew & Gill	1995	Longitudinal Predictive Validity	Paper Presentation
Eno & Woehlke	1995	Predictive Validity	Journal Article
Lang & Chew	1997	Retention Prediction	Paper Presentation
Chew	2001	*Lollipop Test* Head Start Norms	Paper Presentation
Venet, Normandeau, Letarte, & Bigras	2003	Validation of French Translation	Journal Article
Lang & Chew	2007	Trilingual Item Analysis (Rasch Model)	Paper Presentation
Chew	2007	*Lollipop Test-III* (Revised & Updated Third Edition)	Publication

Note: See reference list for complete citations for publications listed above.

REFERENCES

Anastasia, A. (1988). *Psychological testing* (6th ed.). London: The MacMillan Company, Collier-MacMillan Limited.

Ausubel, D. P. (1959). Viewpoints from related disciplines: Human growth and development. *Teachers College Record, 60,* 245-254.

Begras, M. & Dessen, M. A. (2002). Social competence and behavior evaluation in Brazilian preschoolers. *Early Education & Development, 13,* 139-151.

Bereiter, C. & Englemann, S. (1966). *Teaching disadvantaged children in the preschool.* New York: Prentice-Hall.

Blair, G. M. & Jones, R. S. (1960). Readiness. In C. W. Harris (Ed.), *Encyclopedia of educational research* (3rd ed.). Toronto, Canada: The MacMillan Co.

Bolig, J. R. & Fletcher, G. O. (1973). The MRT vs. ratings of kindergarten teachers as predictors of success in first grade. *Educational Leadership, 30,* 637-640.

Brandt, R. M. (1971). The readiness issue today. In D. Hold and H. Kicklighter (Eds.), *Psychological services in the schools: Reading in preparation, organization and practice.* Dubuque, Iowa: Wm. C. Brown Company, Publishers.

Brenner, A. (1967). Re-examining readiness. *Childhood Education, 43,* 453-457.

Centre of Excellence for Early Childhood Development. (2006, April). *Québec longitudinal study of child development: Continuing to look forward after 10 years of data collection.* Vandreuil, Québec: Author.

Chew, A. L. (1977). *The design, development, and validation of an individually administered school readiness test.* Unpublished doctoral dissertation, The University of Mississippi.

Chew, A. L. (1981). *The Lollipop Test: A Diagnostic Screening Test of School Readiness.* Atlanta, GA: Humanics Limited.

Chew, A. L. (1983, November). *Validation of an individually administered school readiness test.* Paper presented at the Georgia Educational Research Association Meeting, Athens, GA.

Chew, A. L. (1985, November). *Investigation of the Lollipop Test as a pre-kindergarten screening instrument.* Paper presented at the Georgia Educational Research Association Meeting, Atlanta, GA.

Chew, A. L. (1989). La Prueba Lollipop: Una prueba diagnostica y seleccionadora de la preparacion para la escuela enmendada [*The Lollipop Test: A diagnostic screening test of school readiness-revised*]. Atlanta, GA: Humanics Limited.

Chew, A. L. (1989). *The Lollipop Test: A diagnostic screening test of school readiness-revised.* Atlanta, GA: Humanics Limited.

Chew, A. L., Kesler, E. B., & Sudduth, D. H. (1984). A practical example of how to establish local norms. *The Reading Teacher, 38,* 160-163.

Chew, A. L. & Lang, W. S. (1990). Predicting academic achievement in kindergarten and first grade from pre-kindergarten scores on the *Lollipop Test* and DIAL. *Educational and Psychological Measurement, 50,* 431-437.

Chew, A. L. & Lang, W. S. (1992). *Validation of the Spanish edition of the Lollipop Test (La Pruebe Lollipop).* Paper presented at the Eastern Education Research Association Conference, Hilton Head, SC.

Chew, A. L. & Lang, W. S. (1993). Concurrent validation and regression line comparison of the Spanish edition of the *Lollipop Test* (La Prueba Lollipop) on a bilingual population. *Educational and Psychological Measurement, 51,* 173-181.

Chew, A. L., & Morris, J. D. (1984). Validation of the *Lollipop Test*: A Diagnostic Screening Test of School Readiness. *Educational and Psychological Measurement, 44,* 987-991.

Chew, A. L., & Morris, J. D. (1987). Investigation of the *Lollipop Test* as a pre-kindergarten screening instrument. *Educational and Psychological Measurement, 47,* 467-471.

Chew, A. L. & Morris, J. D. (1989). Predicting later academic achievement from kindergarten scores on the Metropolitan Readiness Tests and Lollipop Test. *Educational and Psychological Measurement, 49,* 461-465.

Docherty, E. M., Jr. (1983). The DIAL: Preschool screening for learning problems. *Journal of Special Education, 17,* 195-202.

Dykstra, R. (1972). Review of the Metropolitan Readiness Test. In O. K. Buros (Ed.), *The seventh mental measurements yearbook, Vol. 2,* (pp. 1175-1176). Highland Park, NJ: Gryphon Press.

Educational Testing Service. (1964). *Constructing and using local norms.* Princeton, NJ: Author.

Elliott, S. N. & Bretzing, B. H. (1980). Using and updating local norms. *Psychology in the Schools, 17,* 196-201.

Eno, L. & Woehlke, P. (1995). Use of the *Lollipop Test* as a predictor of California achievement test scores in kindergarten and transitional first-grade status. *Psychological Reports, 76,* 145-146.

Ferguson, G. A. (1971). *Statistical analysis in psychology and education* (3rd ed.). New York: McGraw-Hill Book Company.

Gronlund, M. E. & Linn, R. L. (1990). *Measurement and evaluation in teaching* (6th ed.). New York: MacMillan Publishing Company.

Hunt, J. M. & Kirk, G. E. (1974). Criterion-reference tests of school readiness: A paradigm with illustrations. *Genetic Psychology Monographs, 90,* 143-182.

Ilg, F. L. & Ames, L. R. (1965). *School readiness: Behavior tests used at the Gesell Institute.* New York: Harper & Row.

Krus, D. J. & Ceurvorst, R. W. (1978). Computer assisted construction of variable norms. *Educational and Psychological Measurement, 38,* 815-18.

Kulberg, J. M. & Gershman, E. S. (1973). School readiness: Studies of assessment procedures and comparison of three types of programming for immature 5-year olds. *Psychology in the Schools, 10,* 410-420.

Lang, W. S. (1994). Bilingual testing. *Rasch Measurement; Transactions of the Rasch Measurement SIG of the American Education Research Association, 8(1),* 343.

Lang, W. S. & Chew, A. L. (1988). *The predictive validity of the Lollipop Test.* Paper presented at the Georgia Education Research Association, Atlanta, GA.

Lang, W. S. & Chew, A. L. (1989a). *The Lollipop Test norms-technical manual for Head Start children in Georgia.* Unpublished manuscript, Georgia Southern University.

Lang, W. S. & Chew, A. L. (1989b). *Developing norms for the Head Start children of Georgia.* Paper presented at the annual meeting of the Georgia Education Research Association, Atlanta, GA.

Lang, W. S. & Chew, A. L. (1990). *Using the Lollipop norms to answer your educational questions.* Paper presented at the meeting of the Georgia Head Start Coordinators, Macon, GA.

Lang, W. A. & Chew, A. L. (1997). *Improving assessment to improve retention benefits in kindergarten.* Paper presented at the annual meeting of the Eastern Education Research Association, Hilton Head, SC.

Lang, W. S. & Chew, A. L. (2007, April). *Using the Rasch Model to determine equivalence of forms in the trilingual Lollipop Readiness Test.* Paper presentation to the Education Research Association, Chicago, IL.

Lang, W. S., Chew, A. L., & Gill, C. C. (1995, March). *Predicting academic success of promoted and retained kindergarten students from multiple variables.* Paper presentation to the Eastern Education Research Association.

Lang, W. S., Chew, A.L. & Schomber, J. (1990). *An initial study of the Spanish edition of the Lollipop Test.* Paper presented at the annual conference of the Georgia Education Research Association, Atlanta.

Lang, W. S., Chew, A.L. & Schomber, J. (1992). The comparative use of the Spanish and English editions of the *Lollipop Test* : a cross cultural study. *Journal of Research in Education, 2 (1),* 23-30 .

Lang, W.S., Chew, A.L. & Schomber, J. (1992). *The comparative use of the Spanish and English editions of the Lollipop Test : a cross cultural study.* Paper presented at the Eastern Education Research Association Conference. Hilton Head, SC.

Lang, W.S., Chew, A.L. & Vargas, C. (1993). *Rasch model applications to determine the equivalence of a readiness test in two languages.* Paper presented at the Seventh International Objective Measurement Workshop. Atlanta, GA.

Lang, W.S., Chew, A.L. & Vargas, C. (1995) Rasch model applications to determine the equivalence of a readiness test in two languages. *Resources in Education,* (ERIC Document Reproduction Service No. ED 379 293).

Lessler, K. & Bridges, J. S. (1973). The prediction of learning problems in rural setting: Can we improve on readiness tests? *Journal of Learning Disabilities, 6,* 90-94.

Leton, D. A. & Rutter, B. A. (1973). A factor analysis of the Springle School Readiness Test. *Psychology in the Schools, 10,* 293-296.

Mardell, C. & Goldenberf, D. (1975). For pre-kindergarten screening information: DIAL. *Journal of Learning Disabilities, 8(3),* 140-147.

Nagel, R. J. (1979). The predictive validity of the Metropolitan Readiness Tests, 1976 edition. *Educational and Psychological Measurement, 39,* 1043-1045.

Nie, N. H., et al. (1970). *Statistical Package for the Social Sciences* (2nd ed.). New York: McGraw-Hill Book Company.

Nimnicht, J., Sparks, J., & Mortensen, J. (1963). Is there a "right admission age?" *Educational Executives' Overview, 4,* 41-43.

Obrzut, J. E., Bolocofsky, K. N., Heath, C. P., & Jones, M. J. (1981). An investigation of the DIAL as a pre-kindergarten screening instrument. *Educational and Psychological Measurement, 41,* 1231-1241.

Sassenrath, J. M. & Maddux, R. E. (1973). The factor structure of three school readiness or diagnostic tests for disadvantaged kindergarten children. *Psychology in the Schools, 10,* 287-293.

Silberberg, M., Iverson, I., & Silberberg, M. (1968). The predictive efficiency of the Gates Reading Readiness Tests. *Elementary School Journal, 68,* 213-218.

Silberberg, M., Silberberg, M., & Iverson, I. (1972). The effects of kindergarten instruction in alphabet and numbers on the first reading. *Journal of Learning Disabilities, 5,* 254-261.

Telegdy, G. A. (1974). A factor analysis of four school readiness tests. *Psychology in the Schools, 11,* 127-133.

Telegdy, G. A. (1975). The effectiveness of four readiness tests as predictors of first grade academic achievement. *Psychology in the Schools, 12,* 4-11.

Tyler, F. T. (1964). Issues related to readiness to learn. In E. R. Hilgard (Ed.), *Theories of learning and instruction: Sixty-third yearbook of the National Society for the Student of Education, Part I.* Chicago: The University of Chicago Press.

Tyler, F. T. (1969). Readiness. In R. L. Edel (Ed.), *Encyclopedia of educational research (4th ed.).* Toronto, Canada: The MacMillian Company.

Vargas, C. & Lang, W.S. (1994). Rasch Model detection of cultural bias in preschool testing of South American and Hispanic American children. *Proceedings of the Eight National Conference on Undergraduate Research, 1,* 283-286.

Venet, M., Normandeau, S., Letarte, M. J., & Bigras, M. (2003). Les propriétés psychométriques du Lollipop. *Revue de psychoéducation, 32,* 165-176.

ABOUT THE AUTHOR

Dr. Alexander (Alex) L. Chew, Ed.D., is Professor Emeritus of Educational Psychology and Counseling at Georgia Southern University, Statesboro, Georgia. He holds graduate degrees from the University of Georgia, Georgia Southern University and the University of Mississippi, where he earned his Doctorate in Educational Psychology. Dr. Chew was awarded special commendation for his dissertation (a first in the Department of Educational Psychology), and graduated with honors. Dr. Chew completed a post-doctoral certification program in Educational Administration at Georgia Southern University. Before joining the Georgia Southern faculty in 1979, Dr. Chew was employed approximately twelve years in public education in Georgia. He has worked as both an elementary and secondary classroom teacher, school counselor, school psychologist and education administrator.

Dr. Chew was a member of the graduate faculty and exclusively taught graduate courses at Georgia Southern University. He represented his colleagues on the Georgia Southern Graduate Council for ten years. He served as Coordinator of the Counselor Education Program and also assisted in the training of school psychologists. He holds doctoral level certification from the Georgia Department of Education in School Psychology, Counseling, Director of Pupil Personnel Services, and Administration and Supervision.

During his academic career, Dr. Chew held membership in Phi Delta Kappa, a national honor society for professional educators; Phi Kappa Phi, a national academic honor society international; and Chi Sigma Iota, a counseling academic and professional honor society international. He was a member of several professional divisions of the American Counseling Association and the National Association of School Psychologists. He is currently a member of the Licensed Professional Counselors Association of Georgia, having served as a member of their Board of Directors from 1992-1998.

In 2000 Dr. Chew was recognized by his peers as the LPCA of Georgia's "Counselor of the Year." A productive researcher, he has persistently conducted validation studies on the *Lollipop Test* and has presented more than 150 professional papers and/or workshops, many concerning the psycho-educational evaluation of young children. In 1991, he received the prestigious Georgia Southern University Award for Excellence in Research. This was the first time the award had been made to a faculty member in the College of Education. The award was based primarily on Dr. Chew's predictive longitudinal validation of the *Lollipop Test*.

In recent years, Dr. Chew has continued his research and revision of the *Lollipop Test* and its dissemination through publications and national and international presentations. He has maintained a part-time counseling practice and is currently a Licensed Professional Counselor in Georgia. He is Board Certified by the National Association of Certified Counselors.

Dr. Chew encourages other educational researchers to use the *Lollipop Test* in their research and appreciates receiving information about their results. Please send inquiries and correspondence to:

Dr. Alex L. Chew　　　　　　　　　　　　　Green Dragon Publishing
7 Turnberry Court, N.　　　OR　　　P.O. Box 160
Aiken, SC 29803-5647　　　　　　　　　　Lake Worth Beach, FL 33460

E-mail: drachew7@gmail.com　　　　　　　E-mail: info@greendragonbooks.com
(803) 514-2545　　　　　　　　　　　　　1-800-874-8844

APPENDIX A

Sample Copy of

English Edition

Administration and Scoring Booklet

For

The Lollipop Test

This booklet is available in packages of twenty-five
copies from Green Dragon Publishing.

1-800-874-8844

info@greendragonbooks.com

ADMINISTRATION AND SCORING BOOKLET

for

THE LOLLIPOP TEST:
A DIAGNOSTIC SCREENING TEST OF SCHOOL READINESS-IV
(Revised and Updated Fourth Edition)

By: Alex L. Chew, Ed.D.

Name _____ _____

Nationality _____ Sex _____

School _____

Months in Pre-Kg. or Kindergarten _____

Examiner _____

Present Date _____ _____
　　　　　　　Year/Month/Day　　　Year/Month/Day

Birth Date _____ _____
　　　　　　Year/Month/Day　　　Year/Month/Day

Child's Age _____ _____
　　　　　　　Year/Months　　　　Year/Months

SUMMARY OF CHILD'S PERFORMANCE

Subtest	Possible Score	Child's Score	
		1st Testing	2nd Testing
1. Identification of colors and shapes, and copying shapes	17		
2. Picture description, position, and spatial recognition	17		
3. Identification of numbers and counting	17		
4. Identification of letters and writing	18		
(Totals)	69		

1st Testing; 2nd Testing. This test may be administered twice (at the beginning and end of the pre-kindergarten or kindergarten year) as a pre- and post-test, or may be administered once depending on the diagnostic and planning needs of the school.

Interpretation of Scores. See the last page of this booklet and the **Developmental and Interpretive Manual** for interpretative guidelines and suggested score ranges.

GENERAL TEST DIRECTIONS

An Individual Test. This is an individually administered screening test of school readiness, and, as such, is not for group administration.

Setting and Materials. The testing should be conducted in a quiet area as free from visual and auditory distractions as possible. A small table is best utilized for the test materials, which consist of this combination **Administration and Scoring Booklet** and the set of seven **Stimulus Cards.** The only other materials needed are several pencils and an unruled sheet of plain white paper.

(Continued on back page of booklet.)

SUBTEST 1
IDENTIFICATION OF COLORS AND SHAPES, AND COPYING SHAPES

Instructions: Place Stimulus Cards in front of child and turn to **Stimulus Card 1** and say:
"Look this is a picture of lollipops. Look they are all different colors."

Scoring: Score one point for each correct response.

	Child's Score	
	1st Testing	**2nd Testing**

Test Instructions:

1. Say: "Show me the **red** lollipop."
(Note: If child does not respond point to the **red** lollipop and say:
"This is the **red** lollipop," but give no further help on this section.)

2. Say: "Show me the **green** lollipop."

3. Say: "Show me the **orange** lollipop."

4. Point to the **blue** lollipop and ask:
"What color is this lollipop?"

5. Point to the **brown** lollipop and ask:
"What color is this lollipop?"

6. Point to the **yellow** lollipop and ask:
"What color is this lollipop?"

   Turn to **Stimulus Card 2** and say:
"Look at all these different shapes."

7. Say: "Show me the **circle**."
(Note: If child does not respond, point to the **circle** and say:
"This is a **circle**," but give no further help on this section.)

8. Say: "Show me the **rectangle**."

9. Say: "Show me the **cross**."

10. Point to the **triangle** and ask:
"What shape is this?"

11. Point to the **square** and ask:
"What shape is this?"

Subtest Test 1 continued on next page.

Instructions: Place a pencil on the table in front of the child and ask: **"See this circle** (point to the circle)?"

Say: **"Draw a circle** just like this one. Draw it here (point to the space next to the circle)."** If child is not successful on first attempt, give another trial.

Follow above directions with the **cross** and then the **square**.

Note: Before administering these items the first time, the examiner should review the scoring criteria on the back page of this booklet.

Scoring: Score two points if child is successful on either attempt.

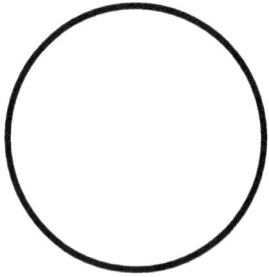

Score: _____

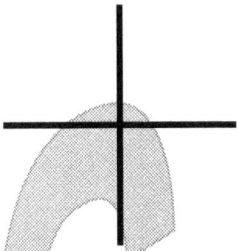

Score: _____

Score: _____

Examiner should check the appropriate descriptors:

Child held pencil with left _____ /right _____ hand

Child held pencil with both hands _____ /with fist _____

Child alternated use of hands _____

Child not using pincer grasp _____

Total Possible Score: _____17_____

Child's Total Score 1st Testing: _____

Note: If examiner is not sure of scoring for any of the above figures, see back page of this booklet.

SUBTEST 1, Continued (2nd Testing)
Use this page for 2nd Testing

Instructions: Place a pencil on the table in front of the child and ask: **"See this circle** (point to the circle)?"

Say: **"Draw a circle** just like this one. Draw it here (point to the space next to the circle)." If child is not successful on first attempt, give another trial.

Follow above directions with the **cross** and then the **square**.

Note: Before administering these items the first time, the examiner should review the scoring criteria on the back page of this booklet.

Scoring: Score two points if child is successful on either attempt.

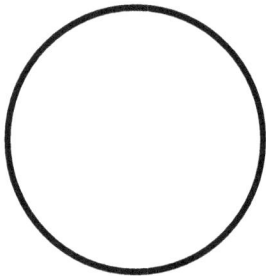

Score: _____

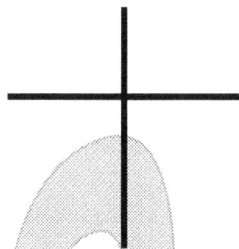

Score: _____

Score: _____

Examiner should check the appropriate descriptors:

Child held pencil with left _____ /right _____ hand

Child held pencil with both hands _____ /with fist _____

Child alternated use of hands _____

Child not using pincer grasp _____

Total Possible Score:	_____17_____
Child's Total Score 1st Testing:	———————

Note: If examiner is not sure of scoring for any of the above figures, see back page of this booklet.

SUBTEST 2
PICTURE DESCRIPTION, POSITION, AND SPATIAL RECOGNITION

Instructions: Turn to **Stimulus Card 3** and say:
"Look at this picture."

Scoring: Score one point for each correct response unless otherwise noted.

		Child's Score	
		1st Testing	**2nd Testing**

Test Instructions:

1. Say: **"Tell me all about this picture."**   (Maximum Score: 5)   _____   _____
    (Note: If child does not respond, ask:
    "What's happening in this picture?")

    Scoring:
        If child identifies "kitties" or "cats," score 1 point.
        If child says "mama cat and kitties," score 2 points.
        Score additional points (up to a maximum of 5) for
        each additional concept the child mentions, e.g.;
        "kitty hungry," "bowl empty," "that kitty climbing on
        mama's back," "kitty playing with ball," etc.

    Probing:
        To improve child's score (if below 5), **one probe** is allowed.
        Ask: **"Can you tell me more about the picture?"**

2. Say: **"Show me (point to) the kitty that is on top?"**   _____   _____

3. Say: **"Show me the kitty that is inside something?"**   _____   _____

4. Say: **"Show me the kitty that is on the left side?"**   (2 points)   _____   _____

5. Say: **"Show me the kitty that is underneath?"**   (2 points)   _____   _____

    Turn to **Stimulus Card 4** and say:
    "See these lollipops? They are all red, aren't they?"

6. Say: **"Show me which is the biggest?"**   _____   _____

7. Say: **"Show me which is the smallest?"**   _____   _____

8. Ask: **"Which one is first?"**   _____   _____

9. Ask: **"Which one is last?"**   _____   _____

10. Ask: **"Which one is in the middle?"**   (2 points)   _____   _____

Total Possible Score: **17**   **Child's Total Score:**   _____   _____

SUBTEST 3
IDENTIFICATION OF NUMBERS AND COUNTING

Instructions: Turn to **Stimulus Card 5** and say:
"Look at this page of numbers?"

Scoring: Score one point for each correct response unless otherwise noted.

___

		Child's Score	
		1st Testing	**2nd Testing**

Test Instructions:

1. Say: "Show me the number **5**."
    (Note: If child does not respond, point to the number **5** and say:
    "This is the **5**," but give no further help on this section.)

2. Say: "Show me the **4**."

3. Say: "Show me the **7**."

4. Say: "Show me the **9**?"

5. Point to the number **3** and ask: "What number is this?"

6. Point to the number **6** and ask: "What number is this?"

7. Point to the number **2** and ask: "What number is this?"

8. Point to the number **8** and ask: "What number is this?"

9. Say: "Tell me how old you are."
    (Note: If child does not know, ask him to hold up how many
    fingers old he is. Ask him to count his fingers. Child must
    verbally tell his age.)

    Turn to **Stimulus Card 6** and say:
    "Look at all the lollipops on this page."

10. Point to box **A** and say:
    "Count the red lollipops on this page."
    (If necessary, add: "Count out loud for me.")

11. Point to box **B** and say:
    "Count the yellow lollipops in this box for me."

12. Point again to box **B** and ask: (2 points)
    "If we added one more yellow lollipop, how many would we have?"

13. Point to box **C** and say: (2 points)
    "Count the green lollipops in this box for me."

14. Point to box **D** and say: (2 points)
    "Count the orange lollipops in this box for me."

Total Possible Score: _____17_____   **Child's Total Score:** _____ _____

SUBTEST 4
IDENTIFICATION OF LETTERS AND WRITING

Instructions: Turn to **Stimulus Card 7** and say:
"Look at all the letters on this page?"

Scoring: Score one point for each correct response.

(See special scoring instructions for item 14.)

	Child's Score	
	1st Testing	2nd Testing

Test Instructions:

1. Say: "Show me the letter **B**."
   (Note: If child does not respond, point to the letter **B** and say: "This is the letter **B**," but give no further help on this section.)

2. Say: "Show me the letter **L**."

3. Say: "Show me the letter **C**."

4. Say: "Show me the letter **P**."

5. Say: "Show me the letter **F**."

6. Point to the letter **M** and ask: "What letter is this?"

7. Point to the letter **E** and ask: "What letter is this?"

8. Point to the letter **S** and ask: "What letter is this?"

9. Point to the letter **D** and ask: "What letter is this?"

10. Point to the letter **H** and ask: "What letter is this?"

    Remove **Stimulus Card 7** from the child's view.

11. Ask: "Can you write the letter **A** for me?"

    Place a sheet of unruled, plain white paper in front of the child and say:
    "Write the letter **A** on this page for me."

12. Repeat the above directions for the letter **B**.

13. Repeat the above directions for the letter **C**.

14. Ask: "Can you write (print) your name?"   (Maximum score 5)

    Using the same sheet of paper, say:
    "Write your name on this page for me."
    (Scoring: One point for each of the first two letters if recognizable.
    Five points for complete name if letters can be read by examiner.
    Rotations are permitted if letters are discernable.)

Total Possible Score: ____18____   **Child's Total Score:** _____ _____

77

1st Testing; 2nd Testing. This scoring booklet has been designed to allow the recording of two sets of scores. The test may be administered at the beginning and end of the pre-kindergarten or kindergarten year, as a pre- and post-test, or administered once depending on the unique needs of the school system.

Administration. The test is especially recommended for use at the beginning and end of the pre-kindergarten or kindergarten year as a pre- and post-test. Used in this manner the test can assist in diagnosing individual student deficits, plan for remedial instruction and evaluate student progress at the end of the kindergarten year. However, the flexibility of the test allows for a number of administration options: (1) at the beginning and end of pre-kindergarten or kindergarten, as a pre- and post-test; (2) at the beginning of kindergarten as a diagnostic and instructional planning aid; (3) at the end of kindergarten or pre-first grade; or (4) at the beginning of first grade in order to facilitate academic and/or remedial planning for individual students, who have been identified with developmental delays.

How to Begin. If the child is not familiar with the examiner, it is essential to establish rapport. Be informal and tell the child that he is going to look at some pictures with you, or, depending on the child's maturity, that the two of you are going to do some schoolwork together. Since the first **Stimulus Card** is an illustration of lollipops, it may help to establish rapport by showing the child an actual lollipop and telling him that he can have it to take back to class (or home) when your school work is over.

Responses and Scoring. Each response that the child gives should be accepted. Mistakes should be quickly passed over without acknowledging them as wrong answers. Do not supply the child with correct answers when he is wrong. Throughout the testing procedure, offer the child encouragement (without giving clues to the answers). When necessary, questions may be repeated as they are contained in this booklet. Should the child experience considerable difficulty on one section of the test, it is permissible to move on to another section. Then, return later to complete the difficult one. Scoring instructions are given at the beginning of each section and at other appropriate points throughout the booklet.

Interpretation of Scores. Regardless of when the test is administered, the primary purposes for testing are the same: (1) to assist the school in identifying those children who will need additional instruction in readiness activities to obtain maximum benefit from their kindergarten and/or first grade experience; (2) to help identify those children who may have special learning and/or adjustment problems and who may need additional individual psychoeducational evaluation; (3) to assist the school in planning their overall instructional objectives and to individual instruction; and (4) in the case of pre- and post-testing, to determine the progress made by individual students during the instructional period. It is not the purpose of this screening test to exclude any child from school entry or to determine that he or she is not "ready" for school. Individual schools and school systems are urged to establish their own local score ranges representing average, above average and below average readiness. However, the child's total score is not as diagnostically useful as the identification of specifiable and teachable units of information and skills that comprise the child's deficit area(s) and require remediation strategies. See the **Developmental and Interpretive Manual for the Lollipop Test** for a discussion on establishing local norms and for additional information on the interpretation of scores.

Scoring Criteria for Copying Shapes:

Circle. The circle need not be completely round, but should not contain any angles. A flattened or broadened circle is scored as correct. Circles not completely closed, or in which closures slightly overlap, are also scored as correct.

Cross. The lines need not be perpendicular to each other and may resemble a large X instead of a cross. However, the two lines must clearly intersect each other at their appropriate midpoint.

Square. The main criteria is that the corner angles be formed correctly. "Ears" or rounded corners are not acceptable. However, the lines that form any right angle may intersect slightly and extend beyond the figure. The figure may not be more than half again as long as it is wide.

© Green Dragon Publishing
P.O. Box 1608, Lake Worth Beach, FL 33460
(800) 874-8844
info@greendragonbooks.com

APPENDIX B

Sample Copy of

Spanish Edition

Administration and Scoring Booklet

For

The Lollipop Test

This booklet is available in packages of twenty-five copies from Green Dragon Publishing.

1-800-874-8844
info@greendragonbooks.com

MANUAL PARA ADMINISTRAR Y CALIFICAR

EL EXAMEN LOLLIPOP:
UN EXAMEN PARA DIAGNOSTICAR EL NIVEL DE PREPARACIÓN DE LOS NIÑOS PARA LA ESCUELA IV
(Revisado y Actualizado Cuarta Edición)

cuarta

Por: Alex L. Chew, Ed.D.

Nombre _____ Fecha _____ _____
                                         Año/Mes/Día   Año/Mes/Día

Nacionalidad _____ Sexo _____

Escuela _____ Fecha de _____ _____
                                  nacimiento Año/Mes/Día   Año/Mes/Día

Meses en Prekindergarten. o Kindergarten _____

Examinador _____ Edad del/a _____ _____
                                  niño(a)   Años/Meses   Años/Meses

RESUMEN DE LA ACTUACION DEL/DE LA NIÑO(A)

Subtest	Puntaje Posible	Puntaje del/a niño(a)	
		1° Examen	2° Examen
1. Identificación de colores y formas, y copia de formas	17		
2. Descripción de un dibujo y su posición, conocimiento espacial	17		
3. Identificación de números y conteo	17		
4. Identificación de letras y escritura	18		
(Totales)	69		

1° Examen; 2° Examen. Este examen se puede administrar dos veces (al principio y al final del año de pre-kindergarten o kindergarten) como un pre y un post-examen, o se puede administrar una vez según el diagnóstico y las necesidades de planeación de la escuela.

Interpretación del puntaje. Véase la última página de este manual y el **Manual de Desarrollo e Interpretación** para las guías de interpretación y las sugerencias de los rangos en los puntajes.

INSTRUCCIONES GENERALES PARA EL EXAMEN

Examen individual. Este es un examen individual para determinar la preparación para la escuela y por lo tanto no se debe administrar en grupo.

Ambiente y materiales. El examen se debe administrar en un área tranquila, tan libre de distracciones audiovisuales como sea posible. Se recomienda el uso de una mesa pequeña para los materiales de la prueba que consisten de **Manual de administración del examen y de puntaje** y el set de las siete **tarjetas de estímulo.** También se necesitan lápices y papel blanco sin líneas.

(Continúa en la última página del manual)

EXAMEN 1
IDENTIFICACION DE COLORES Y FORMAS, Y COPIA DE FORMAS

Instrucciones:
diga:

Coloque las tarjetas de estímulo frente al(a) niño(a), señale la **tarjeta de estímulo 1** y

"Mira, este es un dibujo de paletas. Fíjate que todas son de diferentes colores."

Puntuación:

Registre un punto por cada respuesta correcta.

Puntaje del/la niño(a)

1° Examen   2° Examen

Instrucciones para el examen:

1.   Diga: "Muéstrame la paleta **roja**."
      (Nota: Si el/la niño(a) no responde, señale la paleta **roja** y diga:
      "Esta es la paleta **roja**," pero no ofrezca mas ayuda en esta sección.)

2.   Diga: "Muéstrame la paleta **verde**"

3.   Diga: "Muéstrame la paleta **naranja**"

4.   Señale la paleta **azul** y pregunte:
      "¿De qué color es esta paleta?"

5.   Señale la paleta **marrón** y pregunte:
      "¿De qué color es esta paleta?"

6.   Señale la paleta **amarilla** y pregunte:
      "¿De qué color es esta paleta?"

      Cambie a la **tarjeta de estímulo 2** y diga:
      "Mira todas estas formas diferentes."

7.   Diga: "Muéstrame el **círculo**."
      (Nota: Si el/la niño(a) no responde, señale el **círculo** y diga:
      "Este es el **círculo**," pero no ofrezca mas ayuda en esta sección.)

8.   Diga: "Muéstrame el **rectángulo**."

9.   Diga: "Muéstrame la **cruz**."

10.   Señale el **triángulo** y pregunte:
      "¿Qué forma es esta?"

11.   Señale el **cuadrado** y pregunte:
      "¿Qué forma es esta?"

El examen 1 continúa en la siguiente página.

82

EXAMEN 1, Continuación (1º Examen)
Use esta página para el 1º Examen y el dorso para el 2º Examen

Instrucciones: Coloque un lápiz en la mesa en frente del/a niño(a) y pregunte: "¿Ves este **círculo** (señale el círculo)?"

Diga: **"Dibuja un círculo como este.** Dibújalo aquí (señale el espacio al lado del círculo)."
Si el/la niño(a) no lo logra en el primer intento, déle otra oportunidad.

Siga las mismas direcciones con la **cruz** y luego con el **cuadrado**.

Nota: Si ésta, es su primera vez administrando esta prueba, por favor revise los criterios de puntuación en la última página de este manual.

Puntuación: Registre dos puntos si el/la niño(a) logra hacer los dibujos en cualquiera de los dos intentos.

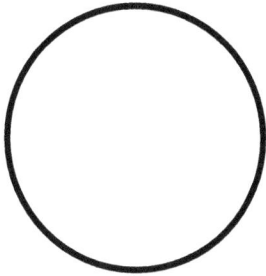

Puntaje: _____

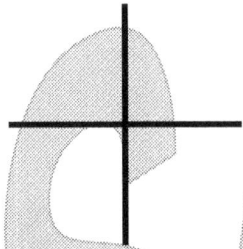

Puntaje: _____

Puntaje: _____

El administrador de la prueba debe indicar los descriptores apropiados:	
Usó el lápiz con la mano izquierda _____ /derecha _____	
Usó el lápiz con ambas manos _____ /primero con la _____	**Máximo Puntaje:** _____17_____
Alternó el uso de las manos _____	
No sujetó el lápiz incorrectamente _____	**Puntaje total del/a niño en la 1º prueba:** _____

Nota: Si no está seguro (a) de la puntuación para las figuras anteriores, vea la última página de este manual.

83

Instrucciones: Coloque un lápiz en la mesa en frente del/a niño(a) y pregunte: "¿Ves este **círculo** (señale el círculo)?"

Diga: **"Dibuja un círculo** como este. Dibújalo aquí (señale el espacio al lado del círculo)."
Si el/la niño(a) no lo logra en el primer intento, déle otra oportunidad.

Siga las mismas direcciones con la **cruz** y luego con el **cuadrado**.

Nota: Si ésta, es su primera vez administrando esta prueba, por favor revise los criterios de puntuación en la última página de este manual.

Puntuación: Registre dos puntos si el/la niño(a) logra hacer los dibujos en cualquiera de los dos intentos.

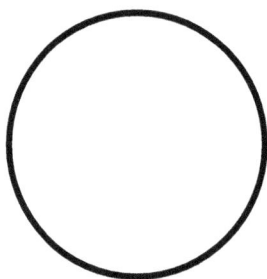

Puntaje: _____

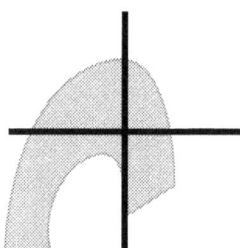

Puntaje: _____

Puntaje: _____

El administrador de la prueba debe indicar los descriptores apropiados:	
Usó el lápiz con la mano izquierda _____ /derecha _____	
Usó el lápiz con ambas manos _____ /primero con la _____	**Máximo Puntaje:** _____ 17 _____
Alternó el uso de las manos _____	**Puntaje total del/a niño en la 1° prueba:** _____
No sujetó el lápiz incorrectamente _____	

Nota: Si no está seguro (a) de la puntuación para las figuras anteriores, vea la última página de este manual.

EXAMEN 2
DESCRIPCION DE UN DIBUJO Y SU POSICION, CONOCIMIENTO ESPACIAL

Instrucciones: Cambie a la **tarjeta de estímulo 3** y diga:
"Mira esta lámina."

Puntaje: Registre un punto por cada respuesta correcta a menos de que se indique otro puntaje.

Puntaje del/la niño(a)
1° Examen   2° Examen

Instrucciones para el examen:

1. Diga: "Cuéntame que pasa en este dibujo."   (Máximo Puntaje: 5) _____ _____
    (Nota: Si el/la niño(a) no responde, pregunte:
    "¿Qué pasa en este dibujo?")

    Puntaje:
    Si el/la niño(a) identifica las palabras "gatitos" o "gatos," registre 1 punto.
    Si el/la niño(a) dice "gata mamá, y gatitos," registre 2 puntos.
    Registre puntos adicionales (hasta un máximo de 5) por
    Cada concepto adicional que el/la niño(a) mencione, e.g.:
    "el gatito tiene hambre," "tazón vacío," "el gatito salta en
    la espalda de la mamá," "el gatito juega con la pelota," etc.

    Ayuda:
    Para mejorar el puntaje del/a niño(a) (si es menor que 5), se permite **una ayuda**.
    Pregunte: "¿Puedes decirme algo más a cerca del dibujo?"

2. Diga: "Muéstrame (señala) el gatito que está **encima**"   _____ _____

3. Diga: "Muéstrame el gatito que está **dentro de** algo"   _____ _____

4. Diga: "Muéstrame el gatito que está **al lado izquierdo**"   (2 puntos) _____ _____

5. Diga: "Muéstrame el gatito que está **debajo de algo**"   (2 puntos) _____ _____

    Cambie a la **tarjeta de estímulo 4** y pregunte:
    "¿Ves estas paletas? Todas son rojas, ¿no?"

6. Diga: "Muéstrame cual es **la más grande**"   _____ _____

7. Diga: "Muéstrame cual es **la más pequeña**"   _____ _____

8. Pregunte: "¿Cuál es la **primera**?"   _____ _____

9. Pregunte: "¿Cuál es la **última**?"   _____ _____

10. Pregunte: "¿Cuál está en el **centro**?"   (2 puntos) _____ _____

Máximo puntaje: _____17_____   **Puntaje del/a niño(a):** _____ _____

85

Instrucciones: Cambie a la **tarjeta de estímulo 5** y diga:
"Mira esta página de números"

Puntaje: Registre un punto por cada respuesta correcta a menos de que se indique otro puntaje.

		Puntaje del/la niño(a)	
		1° Examen	2° Examen

Instrucciones para el examen:

1.   Diga: "Muéstrame el número **5**."
(Nota: Si el/la niño(a) no responde, señale el número **5** y diga:
"Este es el **5**," pero no ofrezca mas ayuda en esta sección.)

2.   Diga: "Muéstrame el **4**."

3.   Diga: "Muéstrame el **7**."

4.   Diga: "Muéstrame el **9**."

5.   Señale el número **3** y pregunte: "¿Qué número es éste?"

6.   Señale el número **6** y pregunte: "¿Qué número es éste?"

7.   Señale el número **2** y pregunte: "¿Qué número es éste?"

8.   Señale el número **8** y pregunte: "¿Qué número es éste?"

9.   Pregunte: "¿Cuántos años tienes?"
(Nota: Si el/la niño(a) no sabe, pídale que le muestre su edad con
los dedos y luego pídale que cuente sus dedos. El/la niño(a)
debe decir su edad verbalmente.)

Cambie a la **tarjeta de estímulo 6** y diga:
"Mira todas la paletas en esta página."

10. Señale el cuadro **A** y diga:
"Cuenta las paletas **rojas** en este cuadro."
(Si es necesario, añada: "Cuenta en voz alta."

11. Señale el cuadro **B** y diga:
"Cuenta las paletas **amarillas** en este cuadro."

12. Señale el cuadro **B** nuevamente y pregunte   (2 puntos)
"Si añadiéramos una paleta amarilla, ¿Cuántas tendríamos?"

13. Señale el cuadro **C** y diga: (2 puntos)
"Cuenta las paletas **verdes** en este cuadro."

14. Señale el cuadro **D** y diga: (2 puntos)
"Cuenta las paletas **naranja** en este cuadro."

Máximo Puntaje: 17   **Puntaje del/a niño(a:**

IDENTIFICACION DE LETRAS Y ESCRITURA

Instrucciones:　　　Cambie a la **tarjeta de estímulo 7** y diga:
　　　　　　　　　　　"Mira las letras en esta página"

Puntaje:　　　　　Registre un punto por cada respuesta correcta.

　　　　　　　　　　　(Lea las instrucciones para puntaje especial para la pregunta 14.)

	Puntaje del/la niño(a) 1º Examen	2º Examen

Instrucciones para el examen:

1.　Diga: "Muéstrame la letra **B**."
　　(Nota: Si el/la niño(a) no responde, señale la letra **B** y diga:
　　"Esta es la letra **B**," pero no ofrezca mas ayuda en esta sección.)

2.　Diga: "Muéstrame la letra **L**."

3.　Diga: "Muéstrame la letra **C**."

4.　Diga: "Muéstrame la letra **P**."

5.　Diga: "Muéstrame la letra **F**."

6.　Señale la letra **M** y pregunte: "¿Qué letra es ésta?"

7.　Señale la letra **E** y pregunte: "¿Qué letra es ésta?"

8.　Señale la letra **S** y pregunte: "¿Qué letra es ésta?"

9.　Señale la letra **D** y pregunte: "¿Qué letra es ésta?"

10.　Señale la letra **H** y pregunte: "¿Qué letra es ésta?"

　　Retire de la vista del/a niño(a) la **tarjeta de estímulo 7**:

11.　Pregunte: "Puedes escribirme la letra **A**?"

　　Coloque una hoja de papel blanco enfrente del/a niño(a) y diga:
　　"Escribe la letra **A** en este papel."

12.　Repita las instrucciones anteriores para la letra **B**.

13.　Repita las instrucciones anteriores para la letra **C**.

14.　Pregunte: "Puedes escribir tu nombre?"　　　(Máximo puntaje 5)

　　Usando el mismo papel, diga:
　　"Escribe tu nombre en este papel."
　　(Puntaje: un punto por las dos primeras letras si se pueden reconocer.
　　Cinco puntos por el nombre completo si el examinador puede leer las letras.
　　Se permiten rotaciones si esto ayuda a descifrar las letras.)

Máximo puntaje: ___18___　　　　**Puntaje del/a niño(a)** _____　_____

INSTRUCCIONES GENERALES PARA EL EXAMEN, Continuación:

1° Examen; 2° Examen. Este manual para registrar puntajes ha sido diseñado para registrar dos sets de puntajes. Este examen se puede administrar dos veces (al principio y al final del año de pre-kindergarten o kindergarten) como un pre y un post-examen, o se puede administrar una vez según el diagnóstico y las necesidades particulares de la escuela.

Administración. Se recomienda específicamente administrar este examen al principio y al final del año de pre-kindergarten o kindergarten como un pre y post examen. Usado de esta manera, el examen puede ayudar a diagnosticar deficiencias individuales en un(a) estudiante, planear instrucción que remedie el problema y evaluar el progresos del/a estudiante al final del año escolar. Sin embargo, la flexibilidad del examen permite un cierto número de posibilidades para su administración: (1) al principio y al final de pre-kindergarten o kindergarten, como un pre y post-examen; (2) al principio de kindergarten como una herramienta de diagnóstico y como ayuda para la planeación de la instrucción; (3) al final de kindergarten o antes del primer grado; o (4) al principio del primer grado para facilitar planeación académica o remedial para cada estudiante que haya sido identificado como un estudiante con retrasos en el desarrollo mental.

Cómo empezar. Si el/la niño(a) no conoce al examinador, es necesario establecer una buena relación. Actúe casualmente y dígale al/a niño(a) que va a mirar unos dibujos con usted, o dependiendo de la madurez del/a niño(a) le puede decir que van a hacer una tarea escolar juntos. Como la primera tarjeta de estímulo es una ilustración de unas paletas, se puede establecer una buena relación con el/la niño(a) mostrándole una paleta real y diciéndole que se la puede llevar a casa cuando terminen con la tarea.

Respuestas y puntaje. Cada respuesta que el/la niño(a) dé se debe aceptar. Los errores se pueden pasar por alto sin contarlos como respuestas incorrectas. No le suministre respuestas correctas al/a niño(a) cuando esté equivocado(a). Durante el examen, anime al/a niño(a) (sin darle pistas de las respuestas). Cuando sea necesario, repita las preguntas tal cual están en este manual. En caso de que el/la niño(a) encuentre bastante dificultad en una sección del examen, se puede pasar a otra sección y regresar más adelante a terminar la sección que presentó dificultad. Instrucciones para el puntaje se dan al principio de cada sección y en otras partes apropiadas a lo largo del manual.

Interpretación del puntaje. Sin importar la fecha en que se administre este examen, las razones principales por las cuales se realiza el examen son las siguientes: (1) para ayudar a la escuela a identificar aquellos(as) niños(as) que necesitan más instrucción en las actividades de preparación para obtener el beneficio máximo de su experiencia en el kindergarten o en el primer grado, (2) para ayudar a identificar a aquellos(as) niños(as) que puedan tener problemas especiales de aprendizaje y/o de adaptación y que requieran una evaluación individual, (3) para ayudar a la escuela en la planeación general e individual de sus objetivos educativos, y (4) en caso de pre y post-examen, para determinar el progreso hecho por cada estudiante durante el período de instrucción. El propósito de este examen no es el de prevenir que un(a) niño(a) entre a la escuela o determinar que el/la niño(a) no está listo(a) para entrar a la escuela. Se recomienda que cada escuela o sistema escolar establezca sus propias escalas de puntajes que representen niveles de preparación de promedio, superior al promedio, o inferior al promedio. Sin embargo, el puntaje del/a niño(a) no es muy útil como diagnóstico pero es más útil para identificar las unidades específicas de enseñanza de información y las habilidades que comprenden las áreas de deficiencia del/a niño(a) y que exigen las estrategias remediales. Véase el Manual de Desarrollo e Interpretación para el examen Lollipop para una discusión sobre como establecer reglas locales y para información adicional en la interpretación de puntajes.

Criterios de puntuación para la copia de formas:

Círculo. No se necesita que el círculo sea completamente Redondo pero no debe tener ángulos. Círculos que se pueden calificar como correctos son aquéllos que sean aplanados, anchos hacia los lados, los que no están cerrados por completo o aquéllos en que los cierres se cruzan un poco.

Cruz. Las líneas no tienen que ser exactamente perpendiculares y pueden, incluso, parecer una X grande. Sin embargo, las dos líneas tienen que cruzarse en su punto céntrico.

Cuadrado. El criterio principal es que los ángulos de las esquinas estén formados correctamente. No se deben aceptar "orejas" o esquinas redondeadas. Sin embargo, las líneas que forman los ángulos rectos pueden interceptarse ligeramente y salirse de la figura. La figura no puede ser más de la mitad de larga como es de ancha.

© Green Dragon Publishing
P.O. Box 1608, Lake Worth Beach, FL 33460
(800) 874-8844
info@greendragonbooks.com

Green Dragon Books Order Form

Bill To: _____

Ship To: _____

_____

_____

_____

_____

_____

_____

Tel: _____ Fax: _____

Tel: _____ Fax: _____

Email Address: _____

Email Address: _____

METHOD OF PAYMENT

☐ MasterCard ☐ Discover
☐ VISA ☐ American Express   P.O./Card Number _____   Exp. Date _____ Signature _____

ISBN	TITLE	PRICE	QTY	TOTAL
1401	The Lollipop Test Booklets (pkg of 25)	$39.95		
4354	The Lollipop Test Manaul (4th Edition)	$49.95		
1398	The Lollipop Test Stimulus Cards	$24.95		
3412	The Lollipop Test Booklets - Spanish (pkg of 25)	$39.95		

ORDERING INFORMATION

Call Toll Free 1-800-874-8844 to place orders via credit card or to bill orders to your account. (International customers call 1-561-533-6231)

Mail orders to: Green Dragon Publishing, P.O. Box 1608, Lake Worth Beach, FL 33460 USA

Fax Orders Toll Free to 1-888-874-8844, 24 hours a day, 7 days a week.
(International customers call 1-561-533-6233)

SHIPPING/HANDLING
For orders under $100.00 net, S&H charges will be as follows:
$6.00 for the first book, and $2.00 for each additional book.

SHIPPING/ HANDLING	
TOTAL